PEDDARS WAY
AND
NORFOLK COAST
PATH

NATIONAL TRAIL GUIDES

PEDDARS WAY AND NORFOLK COAST PATH

Bruce Robinson

Photographs by Simon Warner

AURUM PRESS

The
Countryside
Agency

DEDICATION

To my wife and family, who let me go; and to innumerable walking companions, who made it all worth while.

ACKNOWLEDGEMENTS

The author acknowledges the advice and assistance provided by numerous individuals and the representatives of many organisations, statutory and voluntary. The errors are my own.

Bruce Robinson, now retired, was a journalist for newspapers in Lincolnshire and Norfolk for forty years. He has written or co-written eleven books, including two books on walking, two novels and three titles in a series on Norfolk history, written in conjunction with county archaeologists.

This revised edition first published 2002 by Aurum Press Ltd
in association with the Countryside Agency

A catalogue record for this book is available from the British Library.

ISBN 1 85410 852 2

1 3 5 7 9 10 8 6 4 2
2002 2004 2006 2005 2003

Book design by Robert Updegraff
Cover photograph: The Coast Path near Norton Marsh
Title page photograph: Great Massingham Pond

Typeset by Wyvern Typesetting Ltd, Bristol
Printed and bound in Italy by Printer Trento Srl

CONTENTS

Circular walks appear on pages 43, 73, 97 and 120

How to use this guide

This guide to the 93-mile (150-kilometre) Peddars Way and Norfolk Coast Path is in three parts:

- The introduction, with an historical background to the area and advice for walkers.

- The trail itself, split into eight chapters, with maps opposite the description for each route section. The distances noted with each chapter represent the total length of the Peddars Way and Norfolk Coast Path, including sections through towns and villages. This part of the guide also includes information on places of interest as well as a number of short walks which can be taken around parts of the path. Key sites are numbered both in the text and on the maps to make it easier to follow the route description.

- The last part includes useful information, such as local transport, accommodation and organisations involved with the Peddars Way and Norfolk Coast Path.

The maps have been prepared by the Ordnance Survey® for this trail guide using 1:25 000 Pathfinder® or Outdoor Leisure™ maps as a base. The line of the Peddars Way and Norfolk Coast Path is shown in yellow, with the status of each section of the trail – footpath or bridleway for example – shown in green underneath (see key on inside front cover). These rights of way markings also indicate the precise alignment of the Peddars Way and Norfolk Coast Path, which you should follow. In some cases the yellow line on these maps may show a route that is different from that shown on older maps; you are recommended to follow the yellow route in this guide, which will be the route that is waymarked with the distinctive acorn symbol ♣ used for all National Trails. Any parts of the Peddars Way and Norfolk Coast Path that may be difficult to follow on the ground are clearly highlighted in the route description, and important points to watch for are marked with letters in each chapter, both in the text and on the maps. *Some maps start on a right-hand page and continue on the left-hand page – black arrows* (➤) *at the edge of the maps indicate the start point.*

Should there be a need to divert the Peddars Way and Norfolk Coast Path from the route shown in this guide, for maintenance work or because the route has had to be changed, you are advised to follow any waymarks or signs along the path.

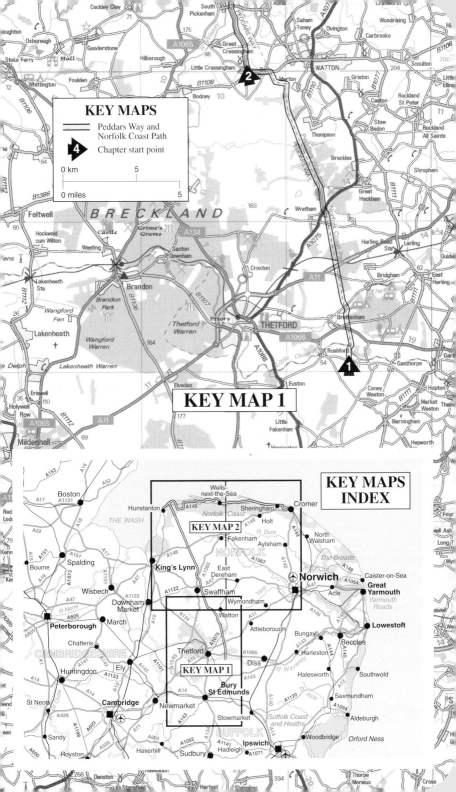

KEY MAPS

— Peddars Way and
  Norfolk Coast Path

◀4 Chapter start point

0 km ———————— 5
0 miles ——————— 5

B R E C K L A N D

KEY MAP 1

**KEY MAPS
INDEX**

KEY MAP 2

KEY MAP 1

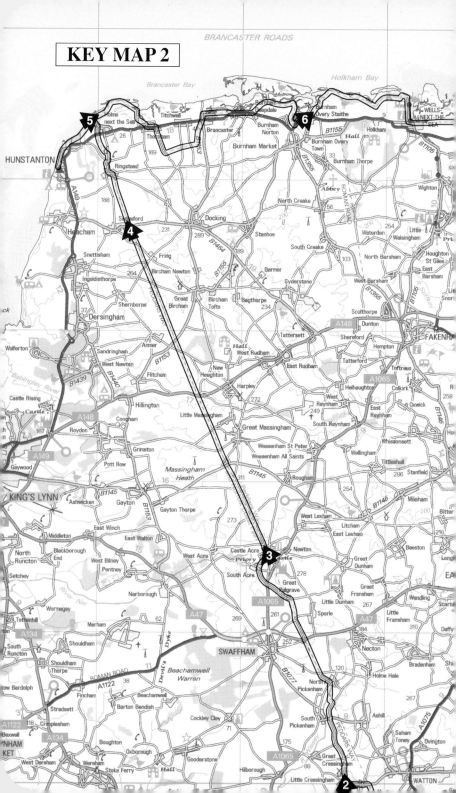

The Ancient House Museum in Thetford – part of a growing town surrounding a historic core and river frontage.

Distance checklist

This list will assist you in calculating the distances between your proposed overnight accommodation and in checking your progress along the walk.

location	approx. distance from previous location	
	miles	*km*
Knettishall	0	0
A11 crossing	4.2	6.8
Stonebridge	2.3	3.7
Little Cressingham	8.0	12.8
North Pickenham	4.9	7.9
A47 crossing	2.1	3.4
Castle Acre	4.9	7.9
Shepherd's Bush	3.5	5.6
Harpley Dams	3.8	6.1
Fring Cross	6.7	10.8
Holme next the Sea	6.0	9.7
(optional: Hunstanton and back)	(5.4)	(8.7)
Thornham	3.5	5.7
Brancaster	4.0	6.4
Burnham Overy Staithe	6.0	9.6
Wells-next-the-Sea	6.7	10.8
Blakeney	7.5	12.0
Cley next the Sea	2.9	4.6
Weybourne Hope	5.2	8.4
(via alternative route)	(4.9)	(7.9)
Sheringham	3.1	5.0
Cromer	5.0	8.0

PREFACE

The Peddars Way and Norfolk Coast Path joins two routes: one ancient (though previously fragmented) and one created with the opening of the Path in 1986. The Peddars Way embraces a Roman road by following country lanes, existing footpaths and recently created rights of way. The coastal path, which it joins near to Hunstanton, runs past marshes, beaches and cliffs on the North Norfolk Heritage Coast which is noted for its dune and shingle flora and prolific bird life.

The Trail's terrain is gentle, which makes it particularly suitable for disabled people, and it contains several lengths where those with wheelchairs, frames or sticks can enjoy a country walk. In addition, a number of circular walks utilising sections of the path make it attractive to day trippers as well as those undertaking longer journeys, and the path is well served by public transport.

National Trails are promoted and funded by the Countryside Agency and maintained by local authorities. They are all waymarked with a distinctive acorn symbol which signals that you are on the right route.

I hope that you will enjoy using this book during many hours of walking through the delightful countryside of Suffolk and Norfolk.

Ewen Cameron
Chairman
Countryside Agency

PART ONE

INTRODUCTION

Gore Point at Holme is an exciting place on a breezy day. Banks of dunes shield the land from view. The sea thunders in, whipped by winds that can blow all the way from the Arctic. And the sky goes on for ever, lending a marvellous sense of isolation.

The Point has an element of symbolism, too, in that it is also the fulcrum of the 93-mile (150-km) national trail – the Peddars Way and Norfolk Coast Path; the place where the Wash turns the corner of the north-west Norfolk coast; and where our routes turn the corner, too. To the south, the Peddars Way lances across the landscape as far as Suffolk, while to the north-east the Coast Path meanders by creek, beach and cliff all the way to Cromer.

The trail is indeed two paths, joined: one ancient and historic, the other relatively new and deliberately created. Together, they offer some fine walking, with some sections of bridleway, quiet roads and tracks that can also be used by cyclists and horseriders.

Beginning amid the forest-strewn borders of Norfolk and Suffolk, following the chalk ridge of north-west Norfolk, and continuing round the North Norfolk Heritage Coast, within an officially designated Area of Outstanding Natural Beauty, history is never far away. Indeed, the Peddars Way is a Roman road built shortly after AD 61. So the walk is a glorious patchwork of heath and forest, popular resorts and former ports, marl pits and agricultural land, cliffs and creeks, sailing centres and nature reserves.

An increase in the number of people enjoying the open air emerged in the 1970s, the rise apparently running parallel with a period of social change, which, in landscape terms, has been almost as significant as the introduction of 'intensive' farming practices during and after the war years. Drawn initially by low property prices and by Norfolk's landscape attractions, newcomers – commuters, urban refugees, retirement or second-home seekers – flooded in. Today, East Anglia in general, and Norfolk in particular, is still one of the least densely populated of all the regions, but one of the fastest-growing.

The effects have been far-reaching. For decades there had been a shift from a traditional agricultural base to light industry, services and tourism. Then, as pressure for housing grew, land and property prices climbed, and the suburbs marched further into the countryside.

Much of the influx has been retirement- rather than industry-led, which has given rise to fears of a top-heavy age grouping. It has also put pressure on local resources and village life, structures often weakened by the loss of schools, shops and pubs, and by reduced rail and bus services. Just as some villages have become puffed up with new housing, others, like many of Norfolk's churches, now stand isolated. The national trail therefore runs through a landscape of perpetual change.

The richly decorated ruins of Castle Acre's Cluniac priory still retain a special grandeur.

The remains of piers and walkways are a stark reminder of Thornham's long-gone days as a busy port.

Initial discussions on a long-distance route began in the 1960s, and in the late 1970s a feasibility study was undertaken for the Countryside Commission by Mr J. F. (Willie) Wilson, a field officer employed by Norfolk County Council. His report was published in 1982. Sadly, 'Willie' Wilson died shortly afterwards. In 1983, Willie's Clump, a small grouping of native trees beside the Peddars Way on the Norfolk Wildlife Trust nature reserve at Thompson, was dedicated to the memory of J. F. Wilson. On 8th July 1986 the route was officially opened by HRH The Prince of Wales in a ceremony on the beach at Holme.

Landscape

Aside from its coastline, which has been open to other influences, Norfolk is a product of successive glaciations that squeezed and scraped the land, smoothed the chalk ridge of north-west Norfolk, deposited wide tracts of boulder clay and gravel over earlier rocks and estuarine deposits, and altered drainage patterns. Movements in the earth's crust and the subsequent melting of the ice caps also combined to raise and tip the area, so that the highest of the rocks can be found in the north-west and the lowest in the south-east, giving the county a perceptible list towards the Low Countries.

Human arrival is loosely dated to about 400,000 BC – although excavations at Hurst Fen, Mildenhall, have revealed indications of earlier incursions – when Norfolk was still united to the Continent by the North Sea basin, a landscape of forest, swamp and freshwater pools. Only in 7,000–6,000 BC did rising sea levels finally inundate the land bridge.

The watershed of the east coast and Wash rivers is the area of heavy soil chiefly derived from boulder clay, a tract that divides the central area of Norfolk and Suffolk and that formerly supported woodland. The massive chalk ridge, which runs through west Norfolk and connects East Anglia with southern England, remains a substantial element. Five to 10 miles (8–16 km) wide, it may have formed a belt of open country to the west of the boulder clay after the Neolithic period.

Wildlife

Norfolk is a mecca for nature-lovers and a paradise for bird-watchers, with habitats ranging from pine-clad Brecks and open heaths to set-aside farmland and a coastline embracing some of the finest sand dunes and saltmarshes in Europe.

The entire 22 miles (35 km) from Holme to Weybourne is designated as a Site of Special Scientific Interest (SSSI) and has received nearly every wildlife bouquet available. The Ramsar (Iran) Convention recognises it as an internationally important wetland, and it is also a UNESCO Biosphere Reserve and an EEC Special Protection Area (for wild birds).

Some of the country's most famous coastal reserves are to be found here – Holme, Titchwell, Scolt Head, Blakeney Point, Cley, Holkham. Inland, there are such gems as Knettishall, East Wretham, Thompson Common and Ringstead Downs.

North Norfolk, in particular, is a region of infinite interest, a landscape constantly in the process of modification by tide and current, offering a rich menu of natural history and wildlife, feelings of remoteness and changing blends of sound, light, colour and movement.

This fragile coastline is also under constant threat from visitor pressure. Fortunately, Norfolk has long been at the forefront of protection. The Norfolk Wildlife Trust, the first county-based voluntary nature conservation body in Britain, was founded in 1926. It now boasts nearly 6,500 acres (2,630 hectares) of reserves.

Peddars Way

In the bloody aftermath of the Boudiccan revolt against Rome shortly after AD 61, Suetonius Paulinus, military commander and governor of Britain, ordered detachments of his troops to settle accounts with the remnants of the tribes of the Iceni who had survived the decisive final battle.

The main areas of what appears to have been an Iceni tribal federation seem to have been Norwich and Caistor St Edmund, Snettisham, King's Lynn and Thetford, north Suffolk, and what was then an island in the middle of the fens where March and Stonea now stand. They were small farmers and metal-workers who were self-sufficient in most of the basics of life and who were ruled, until just before the revolt, by Prasutagus. He was king by courtesy of the emperor, receiving in return guarantees of freedom from external attack and the retention of elements of autonomy.

It was the death of Prasutagus that sparked a major revolt inspired by his queen, Boudicca, and that in turn led to the sacking of Colchester, London and St Albans. That she almost succeeded in defeating Roman military power had much to do with the timing. The 14th and 20th Legions, with auxiliaries and elements of the 9th, were preoccupied with attacking the final stronghold of the Druids on the Isle of Anglesey. That Boudicca failed was due in large part to the professionalism of the Roman soldiery and the insight of Paulinus who, though outnumbered, successfully lured her into a trap.

These were the battle-hardened troops who now harried the defeated survivors with such enthusiasm that Nero, responding to complaints, sent in an arbitrator. Shortly afterwards Paulinus was replaced and the Romanisation of Norfolk began. Military roads were built and the site of a county town, Caistor St Edmund, was chosen. Ultimately, Caistor stood at the centre of a web of roads that reached into all corners of the county.

Peddars Way was one of the earliest roads to be built in the county. Today, it remains as the most substantial and best-preserved of all Norfolk's known Roman roads. Built of local materials to military specifications, it hugs the slopes of the chalk ridge, passes through two of the four known areas of Iceni tribal concentration, and may initially have been used for some form of policing. It probably provided a fast link between the Roman garrison at Colchester and anchorages in the Holme or Snettisham areas.

While military requirements may have faded at an early date, the road has remained a major landmark ever since. It defined many parish boundaries, linked communities and allowed the movement of produce, and has been used over the centuries by peasants and pilgrims, drovers and gypsies.

The name Peddars Way is not Roman and is not exclusive to this road. It seems to be a surviving late medieval attachment, and may be little more than a generic name for a footpath.

Planning the walk

There are $90\frac{1}{2}$–$95\frac{1}{2}$ miles (146–154 km) between Knettishall and Cromer, depending on whether you decide to visit Hunstanton. This Wash resort is an optional detour. For those planning to walk only the coastal section, then Hunstanton is an obvious choice as a start/finish point.

The physical challenge of the trail would be classified by many ramblers as 'moderate'. There are no particularly long or arduous climbs, no rock faces or peat bogs. Instead, the walker will encounter flinty or grassy tracks, forest rides, country lanes, some fairly gentle hills, sand and shingle, sea banks, paths by creeks and marshes, and bracing clifftop sections.

The diminutive Little Ouse River at Knettishall marks the physical boundary

between Suffolk and Norfolk.

Admittedly, uneven surfaces and gradual gradients can be tiring, and the walk is more testing on the coast than on the Peddars Way. But the going is usually relatively easy and the route is particularly suitable for beginners, or the over 50s.

Thus the particular joy of this walk is not necessarily its physical challenge, but the variety of its moods. There is a subtlety about it that can be found nowhere else. Local food, and some marvellous pubs, offer other, more earthly pleasures.

The entire walk has been done in three days, although not by me. If you are a 20-miles-a-day walker, then it can be completed in under five days. Six or seven days is ideal if you prefer a more leisurely pace. By taking time out – at Castle Acre, or one of the coastal towns or villages – then the route can offer the framework for an even longer holiday.

General facilities, such as shops, pubs, telephones and post offices, are in reasonable supply, although easier to find on the coast than on the Peddars Way. The same can be said of accommodation. In general, hotels, guest houses and bed and breakfast establishments are in short supply along some stretches of the Peddars Way, but every town or village on the coast offers facilities of some sort.

There is no obvious best time to walk the national trail. My own preference is for early June, when the vegetation is fresh and the hedgerows are in blossom; but I have enjoyed some wonderful walking in winter. On the other hand, spring and autumn migration periods are an attraction to bird-watchers. During the height of the summer and at bank holidays the coast can become inundated with visitors. If you intend to walk at these times it is essential to book accommodation well in advance.

Waymarks

The primary waymarker is the Countryside Agency's acorn supplemented by routed arrows in yellow, blue or dark red to indicate footpath, bridleway or byway, and also routed wooden fingerposts indicating destination and distance.

Equipment tips

Given dry weather, there is no reason why the walk cannot be completed in strong shoes, but it is not recommended. Walking surfaces are varied (stony paths, grass, sea banks, shingle, cliff tops, marsh fringes, metalled roads) and boots give support to the ankles. In addition, footwear can become soaked if you encounter wet undergrowth. Even a heavy dew on a hot summer's morning can saturate trouser bottoms and feet.

Good rainwear is essential, and remember that temperatures tend to be higher inland than on the coast. It can be sultry in the Brecks, where forest plantations shut out the breeze and hold the heat; but capricious winds chill in seconds in the more exposed areas. The evenings may be cold – pack a sweater.

During spells of very hot weather it is worth carrying drink, as on some stretches of the Peddars Way liquid can be hard to find. Some insect repellent might come in handy, too.

Weather

Artists are entranced by the quality of the light, and the area is famous for its sunrises and sunsets. Sky and cloud form part of the interplay between light and landscape, particularly along the coast, where low horizons lend spaciousness to the scene.

Partly by reason of geographical location, East Anglia possesses a climate that is marginally more continental than the rest of Britain. Average rainfall is comparatively low, particularly in Breckland.

East Anglia is also at the crossroads of four conflicting air masses. Westerlies can bring moist and temperate Atlantic weather; southerlies sometimes carry a touch of almost equatorial warmth; northerlies are occasionally measured in degrees of Arctic cold; and easterlies may bring air off the Continent. Winds between north and east are inclined to bring rain and cloudy skies.

A personal weather forecast is available during office hours from the Norwich Weather Centre on 01603 660779. The Weathercall recorded forecast is available on 09068 111338, and coastguard information on weather and tides on 01493 851338.

Warnings and safety

Common sense dictates that walkers keep out of crops and fields and stay on defined paths. Do not attempt to feed farm animals, and do not leave litter.

Fire is a possibility during spells of dry weather, when forest plantations and grass verges can become tinder-dry. Do not toss empty bottles into the undergrowth, never light fires, and make sure cigarettes are extinguished.

The Stanford Battle Area is out of bounds. It is marked by warning signs, and the section that touches the Peddars Way near Thompson is mostly fenced. This is an active military area, and Army manoeuvres may be seen or heard at any time.

Cliffs are subject to constant erosion and falls. On no account walk to the edge or attempt to climb or scramble on them.

The North Norfolk coast is an Area of Outstanding Natural Beauty that attracts visitors because of its sandy beaches, dunes and saltmarshes. Help support the local communities and the environment by purchasing goods and food locally and making use of the excellent Coast Hopper bus service that runs regularly along the coast. Timetables are available from Tourist Information Centres. When on the coast obtain a free copy of the *Norfolk Coast Guardian* paper.

Norfolk's pleasant coastline disguises the fact that treacherous currents, steeply shelving beaches and a very strong undertow – at Cley, Salthouse and Weybourne, for example – often take the unwary by surprise. Swimming in these areas is dangerous. Brancaster, Burnham Overy Staithe, Wells and Blakeney are tidal harbours, and swimming in the channels is also dangerous.

There are numerous 999 emergency telephones around the coast, including one at Holkham Gap (at the bottom of Lady Ann's Road), and another at Morston quay. At Wells, the nearest telephone is at the bottom of Beach Road, near the café. In an emergency, dial 999 and ask for the coastguards (see Useful Addresses on page 140).

Norfolk's coastal communities and local authorities are also on the alert to deal with the threat of high tides and flooding. If a tidal red alert is sounded, emergency procedures are put into action with police and officials linked by radio to a special operations room at North Walsham.

PART TWO

PEDDARS WAY AND NORFOLK COAST PATH

1 Knettishall to Little Cressingham

over the A11 and through Stonebridge
14¼ miles (22.9 km)

The first few hundred yards of the national trail are not in Norfolk at all, but in Suffolk, and they offer a lovely introduction to what lies ahead. Knettishall Heath **1** (see page 38) is a green and restful backdrop. The wooded river banks and plantation fringes are alive with bird life, and glimpsed from higher ground on the heath the land can be seen to dip gently towards a forest-swathed horizon.

Most of the walking on this section is easy, and the vistas unwind from heath to river valley to forest plantation, and then to early views of working landscapes in one of the most intensively farmed counties in the country.

Begin near the information board at the small car park **A** opposite Blackwater Carr. Before setting off, look for a slight swelling in the ground amid the foliage behind the information board. This is an early sight of the surviving Roman agger (bank) of the Peddars Way. Cross the road and take the path under the trees amid the birch and bracken. A finger-post marks the start of the trail. After 800 yards (730 metres) the leafy path winds right and leads to a footbridge over the Little Ouse River. This marks the end of the trail's brief flirtation with Suffolk.

It is an interesting spot, not least because the river is the county boundary. To the west is Shadwell estate. In 1986 Sheikh Hamdan Al Maktoum, the racehorse owner and breeder, opened the nearby Riddlesworth Stud, said to be the most lavish in Europe. A short distance to the east is Riddlesworth Hall School where Diana, Princess of Wales, was a pupil between 1970 and 1973. As for the crossing point, known as the Blackwater ford, a number of tracks once converged here.

Across the footbridge the path cuts through the trees and follows the edge of the West Harling shelter belt. There is an old parish boundary marker hidden in the grass on the left of the path at the start of the belt, and another further along on the right. In spring and summer the spindle trees here are sometimes festooned with millions of caterpillers and hanging drapes of cobwebs. The scenery here is modern Breckland (see page 40) – shelter belts, plantations of conifers and lines of gnarled Scots pine **2**. Rabbits scamper across flint-strewn fields, and in dry weather giant irrigation systems ceaselessly water the light, sandy soils.

On the other side of the A1066, and over the Thetford–East Harling road, the path enters Forestry Commission plantations **3** at Thorpe Woodlands camping and caravan site (which has a small seasonal camping area for backpackers).

To the left the agger of the old Roman road, now dotted with bushes and trees, acts as a buffer between the plantations and adjoining farmland. The Roman road seems to have been raised at this point, perhaps because of wetter ground close to the river. West Harling, Middle Harling and Harling Thorpe, now Thorpe Woodlands, are all deserted medieval settlements.

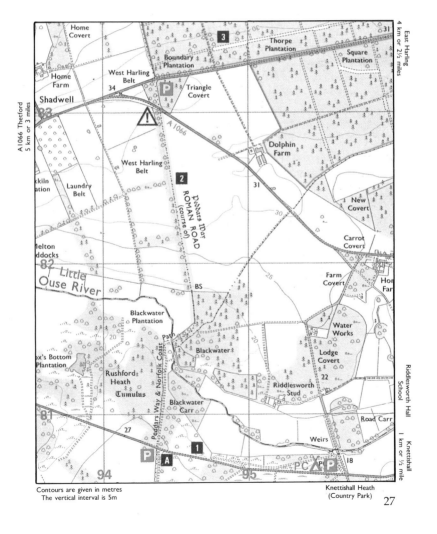

Contours are given in metres
The vertical interval is 5m

Knettishall Heath
(Country Park)

Approaching the River Thet the path crosses the edge of a water meadow and turns right **B** along the river bank. Parts of the meadow can become very wet, but boardwalks have been laid here and along the bank. Once across the footbridge and over the Brettenham road, the path leads into Broom Covert and then alongside fields, hedges and forestry plantations towards the A11, the main Norwich–London trunk road.

Beside Brettenham Heath nature reserve **4** (see page 41) the track crosses to the west side of a wire fence. The walking is easy and the views across the heath are extensive (the reserve is closed to the public). Take care at the A11 **C**. It is a dual carriageway and traffic moves very quickly. There is a waiting space halfway across. Over the road, the railway level crossing on the Ely–Norwich railway line **D** presents the next obstacle. Again, if you use the gates, proceed with caution. If you prefer, turn to the right in front of the gates and follow the path through a low, but safe, tunnel under the line.

The track coming in from the left just over the crossing is the Harling Drove, or Great Fen Road, which probably originated in the Fens. Its age is unknown but it is certainly pre-Roman. Later, it became a route favoured by drovers. Close to the Peddars Way, the Drove Road passes a number of Breck meres, and watering places including Langmere and Ringmere. There is a lack of naturally occurring water in the Brecks, so watering places assumed great significance. Nearby, too, is East Wretham heath nature reserve **5** (see page 42).

A boardwalk aids the walker by the River Thet at Thorpe Farm.

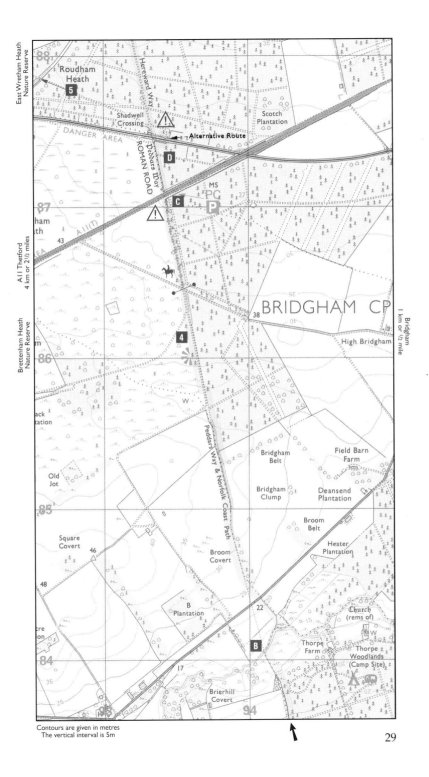

A short distance beyond the gas pipeline pumping station there are faint indications on the left of the old disused Thetford–Watton railway line. There are some pleasant hedged sections and a line of gnarled Scots pine. A short distance over the Illington Road you pass between the abutments of the old railway bridge and then approach a village. The track swings left, then right **E**, and emerges on to the Thetford–Hockham road. Cross the road, pass the post office and pub, and take the left fork.

This is East Wretham, even though many maps carry the name Stonebridge. Both are correct; it depends on which side of the road you are standing. The village lies on the fringe of the military training area and the battle area, and several Army camps are close by.

The metalled road past Brickkiln Covert leads towards the training area, but just past Galley Hill the Army road sweeps to the left while the national trail continues on a gravelly track.

You may see evidence of military activity because, although the battle area is fenced and signposted, there are places where the military can appear on either side of the track. There may also be aerial activity, increased road activity or lots of muffled bangs and flashes. The area is an enigma. It was created in 1942 when the War Department, needing to improve training

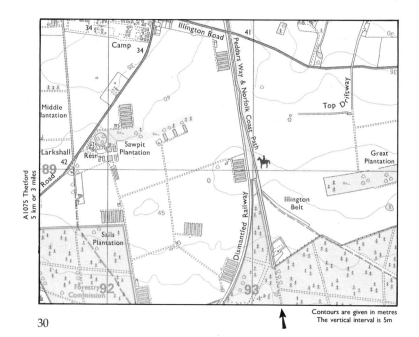

Contours are given in metres
The vertical interval is 5m

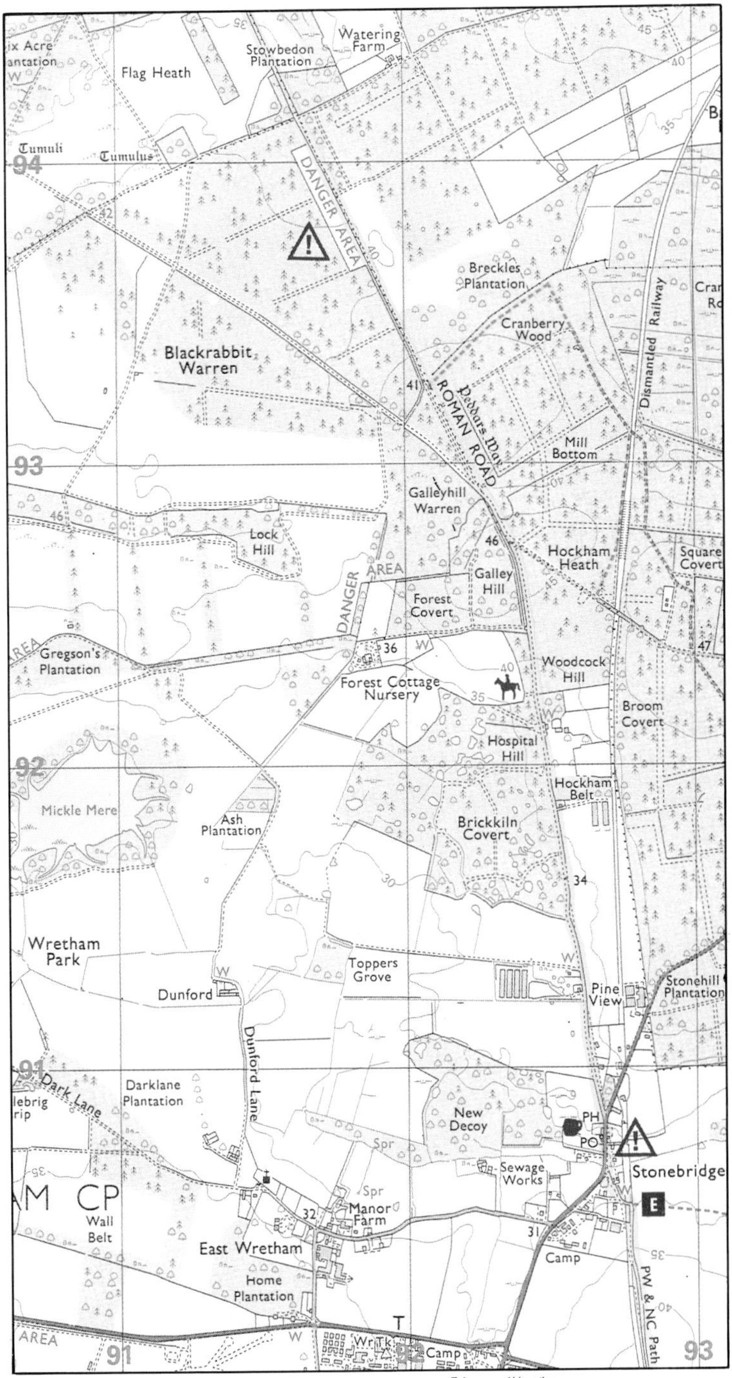

Watering Farm
Stowbedon Plantation
Flag Heath
ix Acre lantation

Tumuli Tumulus

DANGER AREA

Breckles Plantation

Cranberry Wood

Blackrabbit Warren

ROMAN ROAD

Mill Bottom

Dismantled Railway

Galleyhill Warren

Lock Hill

DANGER AREA

Hockham Heath

Galley Hill

Forest Covert

Square Covert

Gregson's Plantation

36

Forest Cottage Nursery

Woodcock Hill

Broom Covert

Hospital Hill

Hockham Belt

Mickle Mere

Ash Plantation

Brickkiln Covert

34

Wretham Park

Toppers Grove

Pine View

Stonehill Plantation

Dunford

Dunford Lane

Park Lane

Darklane Plantation

lebrig rip

New Decoy

PH
PO

Stonebridge

E

M CP

Wall Belt

Spr

Sewage Works

Spr

32

Manor Farm

31

Camp

PW & NC Path

East Wretham

Home Plantation

T

Wretk   Camp

AREA

A1075 Great Hockham
2 km or 1 mile

Contours are given in metres
The vertical interval is 5m

7 km or 4½ miles
A1075 Thetford

One of the many pools in the vicinity of Thompson Common.

and live firing areas, emptied a number of hamlets and evicted about 1,000 people. The area currently amounts to about 17,500 acres (7,082 hectares), of which 2,000 acres (810 hectares) are tenant-farmed. It is home to about 10,000 sheep and, on average, about 90,000 troops a year. Only the churches, fenced and empty, roads and piles of rubble where houses once stood act as reminders of habitation. On the other hand, the area is a wildlife paradise.

Without doubt it is an enigmatic area, and one that produces a constantly recurring dilemma. Should it be returned to the original owners and thus made available for development? Ought it to be designated a nature reserve? At the time of writing the Army appears unlikely to relinquish its hold in the foreseeable future.

Much of the land hereabouts was enclosed in about 1817, and in 1845 a tributary of the River Wissey was dammed and allowed to flood, creating Thompson Water. This was an important stock watering place for drovers and shepherds. Now the secluded lake and adjacent nature reserve – Thompson Common and Water **6** (see page 42) – can induce a quiet and restful atmosphere. Willie's Clump **7**, with its memorial plaque, stands beside the track near the lake. Anyone wishing to walk into Thompson village has about 1½ miles (2 km) to go after turning right just beyond Thompson Water. Beyond the curiously named Shakers Furze there are occasional glimpses between the trees of patches of heath, echoing Breckland's original character.

Over Sparrow Hill the way begins to skirt the edges of Merton estate, home of the de Grey family since about 1337 and currently owned by Lord Walsingham, who facilitated the opening of this stretch of the path. Merton is thought to mean 'the village by a mere', and there are Roman associations with the area. The 17th-century hall, of which the path affords barely a glimpse, was badly damaged by fire in 1956. Edward FitzGerald, translator of the *Rubaiyat of Omar Khayyam*, died at Merton rectory in 1883 while staying with his friend George Crabbe, grandson of the poet. Not far away on the Watton–Great Hockham road is Wayland Wood, said to have been the scene of events that later inspired the ballad and nursery rhyme of the *Babes in the Wood*.

Stay on the defined path across the estate. A short distance past a line of fine trees, including an enormous copper beech, take the track **F** past Home Farm.

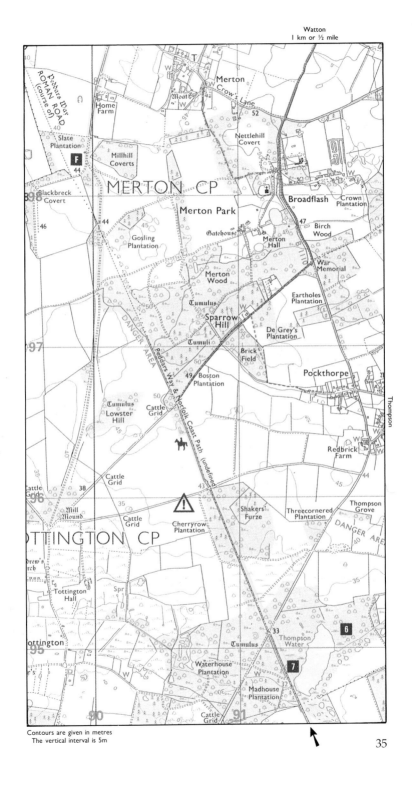

Contours are given in metres
The vertical interval is 5m

A line of giant hogweed – the sap of which can cause skin burns – does sentry

duty on the Peddars Way in Merton Park.

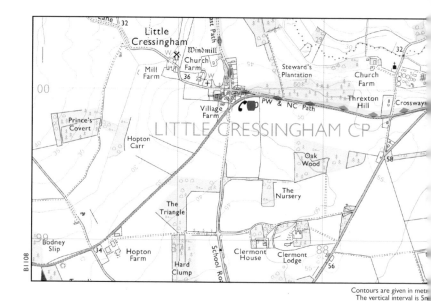

Contours are given in metr
The vertical interval is 5m

At the crossroads, turn left into a green lane, then follow the track right and up to Brandon Road, the B1108.

Watton is about 1½ miles (2.4 km) to the east, while to the north-west the round tower of Threxton church can be seen. This area was once the site of a Romano-British settlement that grew up beside the Peddars Way.

Cross over the road and turn left to follow the headland path along the edge of fields and behind hedges, all the way into Little Cressingham. Turn right at the village crossroads.

Knettishall Heath Country Park

The importance of Knettishall Heath **1** was recognised in 1985 when much of the country park was designated as a Site of Special Scientific Interest by the Nature Conservancy Council (now English Nature). Large expanses of heather dominate the acid soils, interspersed with bracken, grasses, sedges and flowering plants, including heath bedstraw, tormentil and harebell. The park is 360 acres (146 hectares) of heath, grassland and mixed woodland, with a small frontage on to the Little Ouse River. The common lizard and grass snake are resident, and among many birds the pheasant and red-legged, or French, partridge are common. The heath is managed by Suffolk County Council. Facilities include car parking and toilets.

B1108 Watton
2 km or 1 mile

WATTON CP

Long Bridle Road

Field Barn

Brandon Road

Dairy Cottages

Watton Plantation

Sch

Wick Farm

New Plantation

Merton Road

The Car

Merton Common

Peddars Way and Norfolk Coast

Rabbit Plantation

Path

Capp's Bush

Grove Farm

Threxton House

Merton

B1110

90

91

ontours are given in metres
The vertical interval is 5m

A tree-lined walk near the start of the trail at Knettishall.

Brettenham Heath nature reserve embraces one of the largest heathland areas

The Brecks

The modern landscape of the Brecks – one of the driest regions in the country, because of low rainfall and sandy soils underlain by chalk – owes much to human activities. One of the first industrial complexes was at Grimes Graves near Weeting. These were the Neolithic flint mines (English Heritage, open to the public), where more than 1,700 shafts and pits were dug. The area was densely settled in Neolithic times, which led to the gradual conversion of the land from deciduous woodland to open heath. By the Middle Ages the poor quality of the land, much of it grazed by sheep and rabbits, substantially reduced populations and concentrated villages in the river valleys. By this time it had become an open, bracken-filled landscape subject to sand and dust storms. Travellers in the 17th and 18th centuries recorded scenes of desolation – a treeless desert of shifting sands.

Attempts were made to extend cultivation in the 18th and 19th centuries. Much of the heathland was enclosed and many Scots pines were planted to help stabilise the light soils and to improve the game shooting. In the early 20th century more land

remaining in the Brecks.

was turned over to conifer plantations as Forestry Commission operations expanded.

Today, the Brecks offers a landscape of light, marginal land, looming blocks of pines, lines of ancient Scots pine and flint-strewn fields. Bird species include the nightjar, the woodlark and the stone curlew.

Brettenham Heath

Brettenham Heath nature reserve **4** represents one of the largest blocks of heathland left in the Brecks. There are areas of heather and grass, although in some places these have been replaced by bracken and invaded by birch and hawthorn scrub. The diversity of habitats makes it particularly attractive to birds. The reserve is managed by English Nature and leased from the Shadwell Estate Company. Access is by permit only, from English Nature – there is no public right of access.

Thetford Forest

Deteriorating land values and an increased demand for timber during and after the First World War meant that the area was a prime target for afforestation and, in 1922, three years after the

Forestry Commission was formed, planting began locally. By 1937 much of the area was afforested. Today, Thetford Forest is the largest pine forest in Britain, and the largest lowland forest, and is a recreation facility that attracts a million visitors a year. It is also a working forest with an annual timber harvest of about seven million cubic feet (200,000 cubic metres), most of which goes for sawlog production (construction and joinery material). The regimented and sometimes silent plantations, mainly of Corsican pine, are not to everyone's taste, but there is plenty of wildlife. You might spot a crossbill, a magpie or a jay; if you are quiet, one of a tiny number of red squirrel or the more numerous grey squirrel; and if you are lucky, some of the deer that flit like ghosts among the trees, among them roe, fallow, muntjac and the occasional red. The area office of Forest Enterprise is at Santon Downham, a village surrounded by trees and a delightful walking area.

East Wretham Heath

The 363 acres (147 hectares) of East Wretham Heath nature reserve 5, in the care of the Norfolk Wildlife Trust, embrace among other things two Breck meres, and pines planted at the time of the Napoleonic Wars. There are areas of woodland and open heath, and even the runways of an old airfield. The plant list numbers more than 250 species, and more than 130 bird species have been recorded. Roe deer are resident and butterflies are abundant. Access (except on Tuesdays) is off the A1075 Wretham road.

Thompson Common, Carr and Water

This reserve is of great interest to botanists because of the diversity of its flowering plants. Thompson Common and Water 6, in the care of Norfolk Wildlife Trust, is an attractive 309-acre (125-hectare) mosaic of grassland, pingos (shallow ponds formed at the end of the last Ice Age), scrub and woodland. Thompson Water lies to the west and close to the Peddars Way. Coots, moorhens and various species of duck nest on the larger pingos, and the lake is used by wintering wildfowl and waders in passage. The reed fringes attract sedge warblers, reed warblers and reed bunting, and roe deer are resident. Access is from Butters Hall Lane, near Thompson, or from the car park at Stow Bedon. The Great Eastern Pingo Trail, an 8-mile (13-km) circular walk, also starts from Stow Bedon.

A circular walk at Bridgham

5 miles (8 km) approx.

This walk provides a chance to explore the forest and perhaps see something of felling and logging activities.

Start at Bridgham Lane car park/picnic site and set off northwards along the track past ride No. 74 to the crossing tracks. Follow the waymarks with care, because the forest trails can be confusing. Turn left and follow the grassy path into the trees. For a time the path heads southwards and runs parallel with the River Thet, hidden behind trees on the right. Pass the Department of Education (Norfolk and Cambridge) camp site, then turn left along the surfaced camp road, turning on to the fourth track on the right. Turn left on to the Peddars Way and left again just before the road. Rejoin the camp road, cross over the main road, and head for the silo at Dolphin Farm. Swing left immediately when you reach the hard standing near the silo, and find the grassy track leading into the trees. After just over half a mile (1 km) fork left, pass two small tumuli and walk to the road. Turn right here, then cross the road and head left to return to the start of your walk. This walk will take you about $2\frac{1}{4}$ hours.

Contours are given in metres
The vertical interval is 5m

Scale is approx 2 inches to 1 mile

43

2 Little Cressingham to Castle Acre

through North Pickenham and across the A47
11¾ miles (18.9 km)

There is an interesting water- and windmill close to the water on the edge of Little Cressingham; and St Andrew's Church is a dramatic sight. The south-west tower fell before 1781 and only the east bays of the chancel and nave are roofed, though the church is still in use.

Much of the trail from here to Castle Acre is on metalled surfaces, mostly country lanes that ribbon over an undulating and nicely wooded landscape. The walking is easy, if tedious. This is farming country; the forestry plantations having given way to tended fields. The historic line of the Peddars Way, lost decades ago, can be traced on the map only as isolated hedgerows and field boundaries.

Follow the route over the Great Cressingham road and towards Caudle Hill, and cross straight over at the Hall Farm crossroads not far from Pickenham Hall, visible to the west. South Pickenham is an estate village. The Hall was built in 1903 to replace a Palladian house that stood on the same site.

Round-tower church at the privately owned village of South Pickenham.

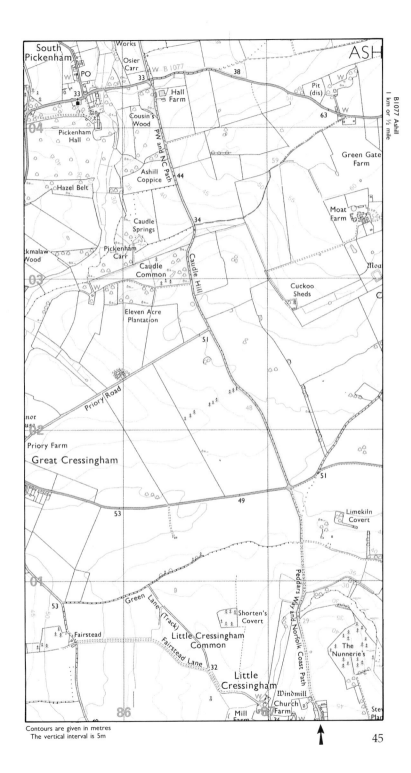

Contours are given in metres
The vertical interval is 5m

45

At Houghton Carr the path moves on to a field headland on the left **A**, behind the hedge, crosses a farm track and then swings sharp left at the next crossing hedge. The path dips down into the valley of the River Wissey, and zigzags right, then left, before zigzagging a final time **B**, prior to emerging on the edge of North Pickenham, beside the school. Turn right towards the village.

Incidentally, there are several stiles on this valley section. The fields are private, and in summer in particular there is likely to be stock in the vicinity.

Before beginning the descent into the valley, a glance behind will reveal the distinctive outline of the old church of St Mary, Houghton-on-the-Hill, recently renovated. North Pickenham can be seen on the far side of the river. The large tower dominating the view is a 350-foot (107-metre) post office relay tower that stands just beside the old Pickenham airfield.

We are now deep into pilgrim country. For decades travellers making their way to and from Walsingham, London and the south passed through this green valley. The Revd L. W. Whatmore, in his book *Highway to Walsingham*, associates this vicinity with the 'Picnamwade' of Henry VI's journey to Walsingham in 1447. He also records that Charles Brandon, Duke of Suffolk, in a letter to Henry VIII dated 1517, said he met Catherine of Aragon at 'Pykenham Wade' and accompanied her to Walsingham. Most likely they turned off the Peddars Way along another Roman road, now disappeared, which branched off nearby **C** to Toftrees and which in the 16th century was known as the Walsingham Way.

The Second World War air base became the home, briefly, of the American 492nd Bomb Group, equipped with B-24 Liberators. It was operational a mere three months, because between May and August 1944 the group flew 64 missions and lost more than 50 aircraft. The RAF took over the base after the war and in 1959 the siting of Thor ballistic missiles sparked anti-nuclear demonstrations. The missile site and launch pads were finally dismantled in 1963.

Turn left at the T-junction on the edge of North Pickenham and follow the road to the junction **C** of the Swaffham road. Cross over on to the grassy green lane known as Procession Lane, which brings you back on to the ancient line of the Peddars Way. Brick remnants of an old railway bridge stand as a memorial to the former Swaffham–Thetford line, part of which you saw earlier on the approach to East Wretham. This section of the railway was built in 1875, but now the rail bridge has been largely dismantled and the embankment bulldozed flat.

The bridge abutments signal the start of a lovely, if occasionally muddy, 1½-mile (2.4-km) walk towards the A47 King's Lynn–Norwich trunk road. Procession Lane – the name is thought to relate to the ceremony of beating the bounds – is wide and hedged, and hemmed in by farmland. At Dalton's

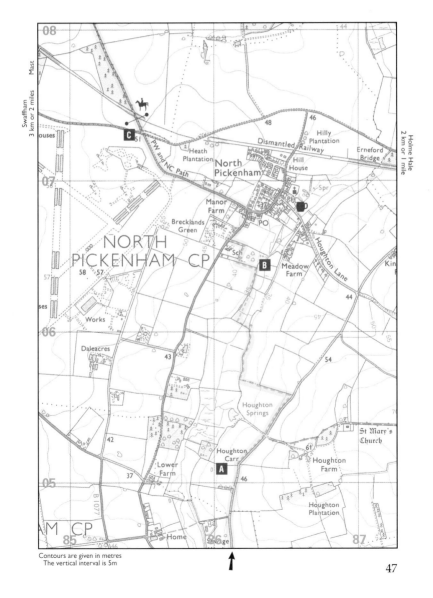

Contours are given in metres
The vertical interval is 5m

Procession Lane, part of the Peddars Way, is thought to derive from the ceremony

f beating the bounds.

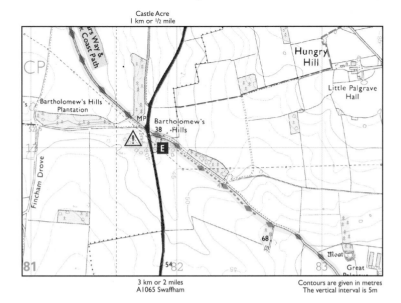

3 km or 2 miles
A1065 Swaffham

Contours are given in metres
The vertical interval is 5m

Plantation the crossroads mark the Swaefas Way footpath (after the Swabian Upper Rhineland immigrants who gave their name to Swaffham), which enables the walker to divert into the town (see page 53).

The distant murmur of traffic on the A47 slowly intrudes. To the east is Petygards, which takes its name from the Petigard family, and nearby is the site of a deserted medieval village known as Cotes, which evidently survived into the 17th century.

Take care crossing the A47 **D**. Follow the metalled surface of the Peddars Way by Grange Farm to its junction with the Sporle road, just over the now disused trackbed of the old King's Lynn–Dereham railway line. The route swings left and then turns sharp right, before turning left again towards Palgrave Hall, from where you walk to the T-junction in front of Moat Farm. The sites of two deserted medieval villages, Great and Little Palgrave, are in the vicinity.

The original line of the Peddars Way is lost here, but it is assumed that it once crossed Hungry Hill before entering Castle Acre. Instead, the national trail turns left and eventually descends along a signposted grassy track parallel with a minor road to the junction **E** at Bartholomew's Hills. A number of roads and tracks converge here, one of them being the east–west Denver–Smallburgh Roman road, known as the Fen Causeway or, nearer to Castle Acre, as the Fincham Drove.

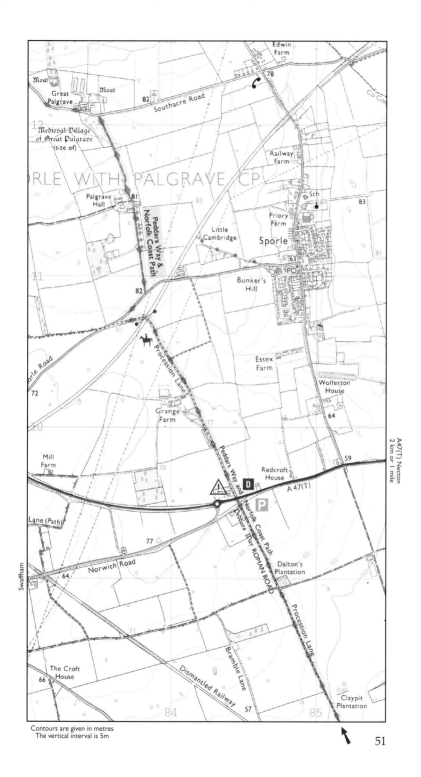

Contours are given in metres
The vertical interval is 5m

51

Cross over the A1065 Swaffham–Fakenham road and follow the sign to South Acre. After a short climb the road bears right and rises to meet another crossroads. There are occasional glimpses of Castle Acre church and priory ruins. Take the lane towards Church Farm marked 'Ford, unsuitable for motors', and cross the River Nar by the little bridge over the ford **F**. Or paddle the ford. This is a lovely, quiet area beside the water, with fine views of the picturesque Cluniac priory ruins.

Once over the bridge, turn right along a narrow lane and enter Castle Acre by climbing the hill by the Old Red Lion hostel, on the right, and passing under the Bailey Gate into Stocks Green. Castle Acre **8** (see page 53) is an ideal place for an overnight stay, and there are good pubs. A tidy, compact hillside village, it is enhanced by its famous castle and priory ruins, a fine church, and by flinty houses. It is also the place where the National Trail crosses the Nar Valley Way regional route.

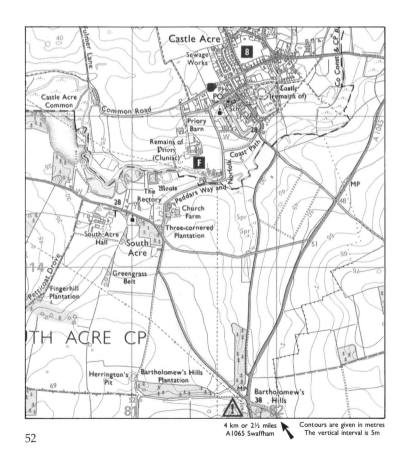

4 km or 2½ miles
A1065 Swaffham

Contours are given in metres
The vertical interval is 5m

Swaffham

Swaffham serves a largely agricultural locality and has a lively Saturday market, including auctions of livestock. Described as the finest Regency town in East Anglia, it was once a fashionable coaching and social centre. Many of the large buildings and houses survive and a pillared Butter Cross, built in 1783, dominates a large market area. The Church of St Peter and St Paul is majestic. Swaffham's most famous son is John Chapman, a 15th-century pedlar who dreamed that fame and fortune would be his if he stood on London Bridge. Once there, he was told that if he travelled back to Swaffham he would find a crock of gold in the garden of a pedlar. He duly discovered the gold and paid for repairs to the church. There is a memorial to him there, and he figures on the town sign. Swaffham is home to EcoTech, the award-winning environmental education visitor attraction. Its 80-metre wind turbine provides all EcoTech's power, as well as nearly 70 per cent of the town's electricity needs.

Castle Acre

Castle Acre **8** holds a dominant position above the River Nar, controlling the crossing point of the Peddars Way. The castle site may date from the Iron Age, but the Normans added the mound. The 11th-century castle was actually built by William de Warrene, the 1st Earl of Surrey, who also built the extensive priory for the Cluniac order. Of the castle, which was extensively rebuilt during the 1140s, the massive earthworks and the Bailey Gate are the most substantial survivors, but extensive ruins of the priory remain and are now in the care of English Heritage. Twenty-five monks once lived there in considerable style, and in 1500 the prior built himself a fine residence, but in 1536 all was swept away by the Dissolution. The Church of St James has some graceful window tracery, and the wooden pulpit is painted with the Four Doctors of the Church – Augustine, Gregory, Ambrose and Jerome.

Churches in the landscape

For centuries the essential elements of the Norfolk landscape have included fields, trees, villages and churches. It remains true even today, for Norfolk still has more medieval churches than any other county of comparable size.

Christianity seems to have reached the area during the 2nd century AD. One of the first Christian East Anglian kings was Raedwald, ruler of southern Britain from 610 to 624, whose seat

The ruins of a Saxon tower and former Augustinian priory give Weybourne

was at Rendlesham in Suffolk and who may have been commemorated by the Sutton Hoo ship burial. Raedwald was converted about 616, and his son, Sigbert, further encouraged Christianity after his accession. St Felix, sent into the area by Sigbert, remained bishop of East Anglia for 17 years. The first church in the county, dedicated to St Felix, may have been at Babingley, near King's Lynn, although the present church there is medieval. In 631 the Irish mystic St Furzey was given a site for a monastery at Burgh Castle, near Great Yarmouth, and by 680 Christianity was so well established that it was decided to divide the see of East Anglia. By 803 the northern half was sited at 'Elmham', probably North Elmham, near East

church an unusual outline.

Dereham. In 1096 Bishop Herbert de Losinga laid the foundation stone of Norwich cathedral, and inspired the construction of many others.

During the 11th century Saxon masons began to build round-towered churches, possibly due to a lack of large local stone. Sometimes, too, they incorporated pieces of Roman brick. The main period of construction was between the 13th and 15th centuries, and many fine examples remain. Several features are peculiar to the region: round towers, flint flush-work and wooden roofs. Many churches now seem to stand alone and isolated. Plague, worked-out land, and shrunken or deserted villages are at the heart of the explanation.

3 Castle Acre to Sedgeford

via Shepherd's Bush and Harpley Dams
14¼ miles (22.9 km)

This is the most straightforward section of the Peddars Way, which maintains a persistent line for most of the rest of the journey to the coast. Much of it is on a grassy, stony track with a few short sections of metalled road. It provides a good walk amid open agricultural landscape as the trail rolls on towards the coast. Ringstead is now the only community of any size that you will touch between Castle Acre and the sea. Before the best walking sections can be reached, however, there is a 2¾-mile (4.4-km) uphill stretch of road to be overcome.

Leave Castle Acre by the Great Massingham road and stay on the pavement for as long as possible. The problem with this stretch – a tiring grind at the best of times – is that the road is not very wide.

The need to walk the entire length on the road has been partially alleviated by headland and verge paths. A short distance from Stone Barn, at a point where a minor road branches left **A**, a specially created footpath runs behind the hedge parallel with the road all the way to Old Wicken Cottages **B**. The headland path ends near the cottages. Climb the stile over the railings and back on to the road. At the point where the road dips there is a verge path on the west side, which continues to the crossroads, where it switches to the east side.

A commanding view from the excavated keep of Castle Acre castle.

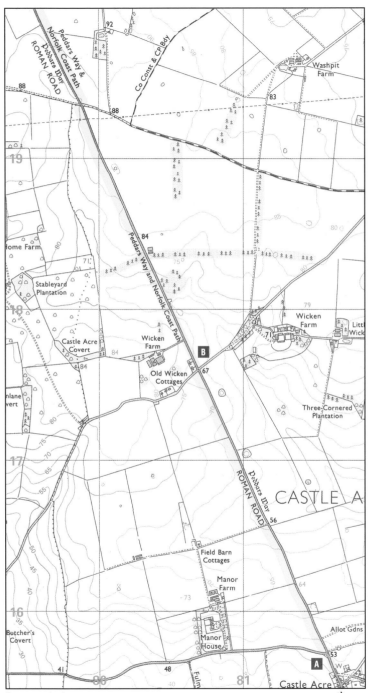

Contours are given in metres
The vertical interval is 5m

57

St Mary's Church and a pond dominate this view of the pretty village of Great Massingham.

Traffic conditions can be dangerous, so stay on the verge. It is now an uphill trudge to Shepherd's Bush, a name omitted from some maps, but the place where the main road swings right towards Great Massingham, while the grassy Peddars Way maintains its forward momentum. Shepherd's Bush, one of the highest points on the Norfolk stretch of the Way, but still only 302 feet (92 metres) above sea level, is also marked by an old Ordnance Survey triangulation point.

To the north are the sister villages of Great Massingham **9** and Little Massingham **10** (see page 67) while a mile or two to the west is the theoretical line of the Icknield Way (see page 70), old even before the Romans came.

Once again the path takes on the aspect of a grassy farm track. Over the Gayton–Litcham road by Rhubarb Cottage it briefly adopts an uneven metalled surface before becoming a stony track, and then offering easier walking with an earthy, smoother surface. The fields here represent a comparatively new landscape. Between 1938 and 1942 some 1,600 acres (650 hectares) of Harpley Common and Massingham Heath and Common were cleared of gorse and bracken, and by deep ploughing, manuring and heavy liming were made to produce cereal crops. Lucerne was also grown, and a lucerne meal factory opened briefly at South Acre.

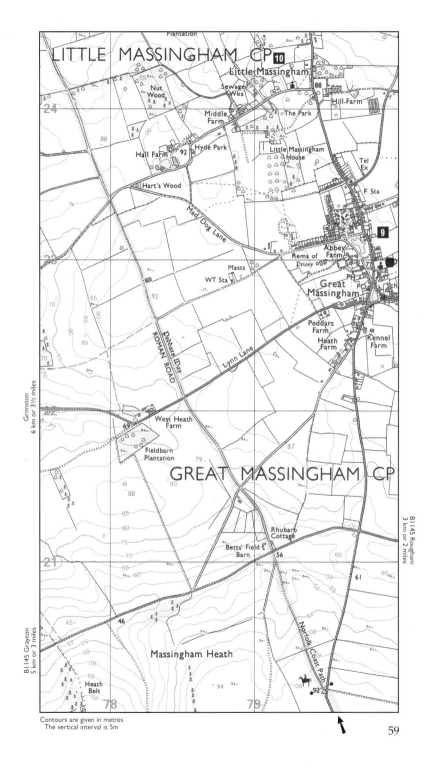

LITTLE MASSINGHAM CP **10**

Plantation

Little Massingham

Sewage Wks

Nut Wood

88

Hill Farm

Middle Farm

The Park

Hall Farm

92

Hyde Park

Little Massingham House

Tel Ex

Hart's Wood

Mad Dog Lane

F Sta

9

Rems of Priory

Abbey Farm

PH

Masts

WT Sta

Great Massingham

PO

Sch

92

Peddars Farm

Roman Road

Peddars Way

Lynn Lane

Heath Farm

Kennel Farm

Grimston 6 km or 3½ miles

West Heath Farm

Fieldbarn Plantation

79

88

GREAT MASSINGHAM CP

B1145 Rougham 3 km or 2 miles

Rhubarb Cottage

56

Betts' Field Barn

60

61

21

46

Norfolk Coast Path

B1145 Grayton 5 km or 3 miles

Massingham Heath

Heath Belt

94

92

78

79

Contours are given in metres
The vertical interval is 5m

59

Past Cockyhoop Cottage the trail dips towards the A148 at Harpley Dams **C**. Castle Rising (see page 71) is a few miles to the west. Now there is in quick succession a fuel pipeline installation (the white 'hurdles' in neighbouring fields are pipeline markers, not stiles) and a clutch of buildings beside the disused King's Lynn–Fakenham railway, which include the former crossing-keeper's house. The line closed in 1953. There is a tenuous link between the old railway and the pipeline complex in that during the Second World War the sidings were used as a petrol dump serving the nearby Massingham airfield.

The original meaning of the name Harpley Dams is hard to pinpoint, although the first word reflects the nearby village. The second would seem to allude either to water, or the distribution of water, perhaps for stock; or to sheep; 'dam' being the word for a mother sheep. A correspondent told me that his grandfather – born near Harpley Common in 1858 – and his great-grandfather were both shepherds, one of them at Holkham, and that sheep were a regular sight on the common.

Use great care crossing the A148 because this is a busy road. Past Harpley Dams Cottages there is a short, sharp climb towards Harpley Common and the start of a particularly nice stretch of the Peddars Way. Now the track becomes increasingly remote, passing through an area of cropped fields, wide skies and occasional lengths of fine hedgerow. Sometimes in summer it seems that the only things moving are rabbits, skylarks and a solitary farm vehicle. The surface is occasionally uneven but it is invariably grassy and the walking is easy.

A distinctive feature of the landscape is the number of marl pits. A creation of the 18th-century agricultural 'improvers', marl was spread on the fields to improve the condition of the light soils. There are said to be 50 such pits near the track between Harpley Dams and Anmer. Some are distinguishable in the fields as clumps of trees or bushes. Others, ploughed out years ago, have left shallow depressions in the land.

Closer to the Anmer–Houghton road small clusters of Bronze Age tumuli dot the fields on both sides of the Way. They are protected from the plough, and would originally have been much larger than they are today. One or two, however, are also covered with trees or bushes, and at a distance can be mistaken for marl pits, or vice versa.

As you walk, you converge with the line of trees to the east, marking the edge of Houghton Hall estate **11** (see page 72).

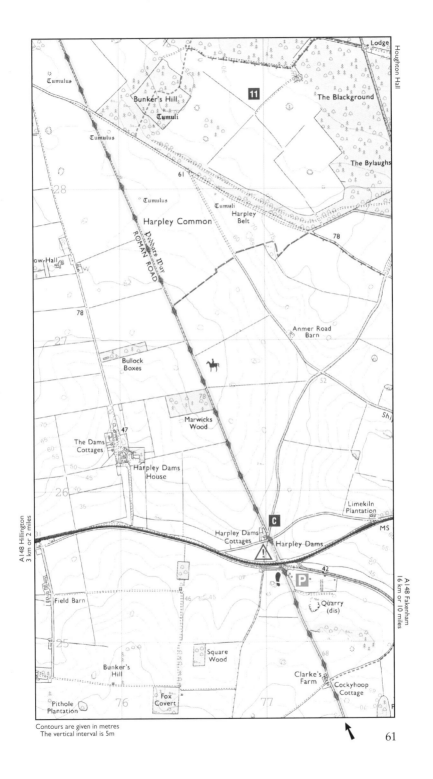

Lodge

The Blackground

11

Bunker's Hill

Tumuli

Tumulus

Tumulus

The Bylaughs

61

Tumulus

Harpley Common

Harpley Belt

78

Peddars Way ROMAN ROAD

ow-Hall

78

Anmer Road Barn

52

Bullock Boxes

Marwicks Wood

47

The Dams Cottages

Sh

Harpley Dams House

Limekiln Plantation

MS

Harpley Dams Cottages

Harpley Dams

C

42

Field Barn

Quarry (dis)

Square Wood

Clarke's Farm

Cockyhoop Cottage

Bunker's Hill

Fox Covert

Pithole Plantation

76

77

A148 Hillington 3 km or 2 miles

A148 Fakenham 16 km or 10 miles

Contours are given in metres
The vertical interval is 5m

61

Anmer village is a short distance to the west and the Royal estate of Sandringham (see page 70) is just over 4 miles (6.4 km) away. Over the road is a triangular-shaped field known as Anmer Minque. The meaning is lost, but it is thought to refer to broken, stony or bumpy ground, something that may be familiar to seamen who recall the dangerous reef near the Channel Islands known as Les Minquiers.

The Peddars Way seems to have retained much of its original width here and one stretch, not far from Great Bircham, is lined with bracken-covered verges and high hedges. This is an area much favoured for picnics.

Further on, the white-capped outline of Bircham windmill gleams in the sun towards the east. Now restored, it has working machinery and a tea room and offers seasonable opening times for the public. Beyond the mill the outline of a cluster of cranes can be seen in the distance. They mark the former Bircham Newton airfield, now a construction industry training school. In this vicinity it is possible to see the effects of set-aside farmland and newly designated wildlife areas.

Bircham's restored windmill seen across harvest-laden fields near the Peddars Way.

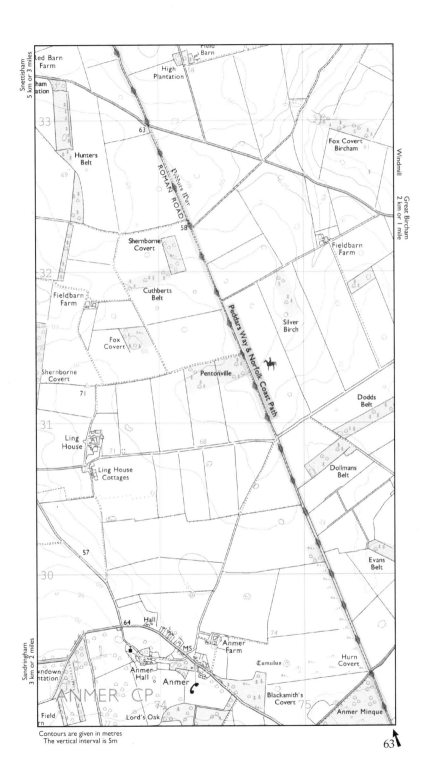

Contours are given in metres
The vertical interval is 5m

On the last lap before the sea, the Peddars Way begins its descent to Fring Cross.

There are high, wide views as the path pushes towards the coast and the village of Fring appears to emerge out of the trees and folds of the hills. The road dips and rises like a switchback as it makes a final approach to what is known as Fring Cross **12**. As the path drops towards the old ford, where once there was a cross, it is worth looking ahead to the distant hill to see the line of the Roman road marked by a long hedgerow snaking up and across the fields.

Sedgeford, $1\frac{1}{2}$ miles (2.4 km) to the west, offers a first glimpse of the distinctive gingery carstone, popular in north-west Norfolk, which contrasts as a building material with the more widespread flint and comes to an architectural climax in New Hunstanton. It is between Sedgeford and Snettisham that remarkable Iron Age torcs made of an alloy of gold and silver have been found (see page 72). Further to the west are Heacham and Caley Mill, the home of Norfolk lavender.

Beside the road at Fring Cross **12** is the old ford. This is actually the Heacham River, which rises in Fring and, fed by springs, passes under the Sedgeford road and over the Peddars Way on its way to Caley Mill and the sea. It is an interesting link because the lavender industry was once based in Fring. In summer, the ford is often either bone dry or little more than a patch of damp grass. At other times there may be a little water, when the approaches will be wet and muddy. In anticipation of deluges, a small crossing point has been built on the right side of the track near the edge of the road.

Caley Mill, Heacham, is the source of Norfolk lavender.

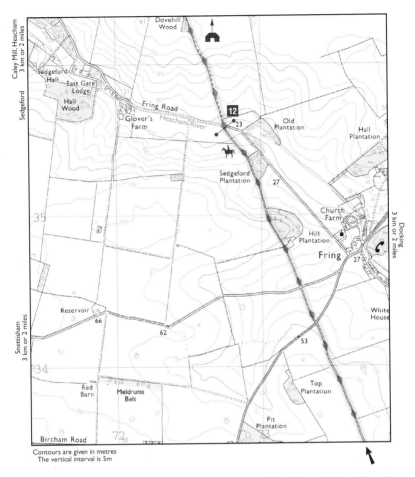

Contours are given in metres
The vertical interval is 5m

If you want to take a break here, walk along Fring Road westwards into Sedgeford. An alternative place to stay is the bunkhouse barn at Courtyard Farm, Ringstead (see page 135).

Great and Little Massingham

In Great Massingham **9**, 18th- and 19th-century cottages circle a spacious green, dotted with ponds, which may have been associated with an Augustinian priory founded in the 13th-century. St Mary's Church, also at the heart of the village, has a notable south porch, rebuilt in 1863 but essentially 13th-century. St Andrew's, Little Massingham **10**, has a 14th-century tower and a roof that looks deceptively old but is, in fact, modern. Just outside Little Massingham is Massingham St Mary, a religious retreat.

A field of oilseed rape marks the road out of Castle Acre.

Agriculture

The Norfolk landscape has been shaped by humans for about 5,000 years, and by the end of the Neolithic period the area was firmly established as a region of farmers and stock-breeders. By 1000 BC Bronze Age communities were living surrounded by grazing herds and flocks, ploughed fields and hedgerows. During the Iron Age the higher ground of the chalk and Breck was of little use for arable farming, so sheep and cattle tended to dominate. Early forms of corn, including emmer and spelt (varieties of wheat), were grown along with barley, which was also grown in abundance by Roman land-owners, who enjoyed the fruits of a landscape divided into enormous estates and small farms. Wheat was grown, with small quantities of rye and oats, and root crops like turnips and mangolds.

Sheep were introduced on a considerable scale in the 15th and 17th centuries, during which period the economies of

many villages collapsed because of social change, industrial pressure, the ambition of landowners, sickness and exhaustion of the soil. Between about 1720 and 1840 the enclosures affected thousands of acres, and many more acres were brought under the plough, and trees and hedgerows planted. The Agrarian Revolution began in Norfolk largely through the ideas and enthusiasm of Thomas Coke (pronounced Cook) of Holkham and Viscount 'Turnip' Townsend of Raynham. It was Coke who adopted the idea of the Norfolk four-course crop rotation, which gave greater yields and reduced pests and disease. In the new 'closed' fields farmers spread manure from their livestock with marl or clay dug from small pits.

The introduction of steam engines in the latter half of the 19th century enabled drainage schemes to be undertaken on a larger scale. Sugar beet factories arrived in the 1920s, and the Second World War saw an even greater acceleration towards mechanisation. Farming has had good and bad periods, the fields have got bigger, and pension funds and finance houses have moved into land ownership. Today we have set-aside land schemes and the conversion of some farmland to alternative uses, such as golf courses and forestry. Norfolk is still one of the best-husbanded areas in the country, and it has produced a rich palette of colours. Pale yellow cereals contrast with red-pantiled barns, the grey of a distant church, and the deep green of a plantation. Brilliant yellow crops are more likely to be oilseed rape (used for margarine and lubricating oil) than mustard, and the pale blue fields that from a distance resemble patches of water are likely to be either flax, grown for linseed, or borage, according to the time of year.

The Icknield Way

The backbone of East Anglia is the great chalk ridge that sweeps in from beyond the Thames Valley towards Hunstanton. This higher ground provided an early corridor of communication, and a series of trackways generically known as the Icknield Way slowly developed. Its actual origins may have been in animal migration routes about 8000 BC, but the Way was certainly in use during the Neolithic period. Goods, including the products of local flint industries, were traded over very great distances.

There are many unknown factors. The Way may not have reached the sea, for there is no evidence of it beyond Ringstead. Again, it is unlikely to have been a single track, but rather a network of tracks used according to ground conditions. Between Gayton Thorpe and Grimston, for example, the Icknield seems to have had one 'all-weather' track slightly to the east of a 'summer' track. North of the River Nar the accepted line of the Way appears to have little connection with the distribution of Iron Age finds, which has led to speculation that the accepted route is a post-Roman distortion caused by the Saxon town of Thetford, and that the Way's pre-Roman course was actually further west, along the fen edge. Some of Norfolk's Icknield tracks were used by the Romans, who farmed extensively in the area and built villas along its course.

Sandringham House

Sandringham house and grounds, which are open except when a member of the Royal family is in residence, were purchased in 1861 for Albert Edward, Prince of Wales, later Edward VII. The sandy habitat, now extensively planted with stabilising conifers, was ideal for game birds, and the original

Sandringham House and estate is the much-loved Norfolk home of the Royal family.

Georgian house was demolished and replaced in the 1870s by a new house of red brick and stone in the Jacobean style. There are gardens, masses of rhododendrons, a museum of motor cars and nature trails. Uncharitable observers have described the house as looking like a grandiose Victorian hotel, and in truth it does; but it has an informal atmosphere and has been a favourite of several generations of the Royal family. Much of the land around Sandringham is owned by the estate.

Castle Rising

Castle Rising was once connected to the sea, and Havengate Lane may have had a wharf. In 1138 William d'Albini built his castle on a high mound to the south, and the street plan suggests that the village may have been laid out at about the same time. The d'Albini castle (English Heritage) has a long and famous history. Its fine windows and many fireplaces help it to retain the look of a rather elegant residence. In 1330, Queen Isabella was imprisoned here, and from 1544 it was owned by the Dukes of Norfolk and used as a hunting lodge. On the green not far from the Norman Church of St Lawrence is a 15th-century cross. Another point of interest is Trinity Hospital, a row of 17th-century almshouses.

Houghton Hall

Built in the 1730s for Sir Robert Walpole, the first Prime Minister of England, Houghton Hall is a fine example of the neo-Palladian style. The original village was pulled down and re-located to the south of the estate 11 in the 1720s, when the park was being landscaped. The house was later modified and made more opulent by James Gibbs, who added domes and Venetian windows. Many of the original furnishings and decorations by William Kent remain, particularly in the huge Stone Hall and the State Rooms. Houghton is the most magnificent house in Norfolk, rivalled only by Holkham, and it has a park grazed by deer. It is open to the public at certain times.

The torc trade

Torcs, from the Latin word meaning 'twisted', were fashionable in the Bronze Age and the tradition was carried on for many years. They were heavy rings of precious metal – sometimes gold, sometimes silver, but usually electrum, a mixture of the two. They were made from wires or bars, twisted together, finished with decorated ends, and probably worn around the neck as a symbol of wealth or authority. The area around Snettisham has produced many hundreds of torcs, or fragments of torcs, over the last 50 years, one of the most famous hoards being originally discovered by local man Cecil Hodder in 1990. Subsequent excavation of the site unearthed 112 complete or fragmented torcs, over 100 gold and silver alloy ingots, and over 170 coins dating from between 70 and 50 BC. It was the largest hoard of gold and silver treasure ever found in Britain. As there is evidence of precious-metal working in the Snettisham and Sedgeford areas some 700 or 800 years earlier, in the Bronze Age, this may have been a metal-working centre of very long standing. The number of hoards found over the years has also led to the theory that the site may have been some sort of Iron Age tribal treasury or bank.

A CIRCULAR WALK AT HARPLEY
3½ miles (5.6 km)

This walk provides a good opportunity to see something of the farmlands characteristic of mid-Norfolk. Park on the hard-standing beside the pipeline installation at Harpley Dams and take the lane to Massingham. Turn right where tracks cross the Massingham road and enter a green lane, tree-lined on one side. About halfway to Cockyhoop Cottage skirt the edge of a field, keeping the hedge to your right. At the cottage, turn left on to the Peddars Way; then right on to another grassy track that runs between the fields. When you lose sight of the track keep on along the edge of the field, again with the hedge on your right. Turn right at the edge of a wood on to another narrow green track which later widens and opens out. This is a fine stretch of walking across open country which continues most of the way back to Harpley Dams. Rejoin your car by walking the short distance on the old trackbed. This walk will take you about 1½ hours.

Contours are given in metres
The vertical interval is 5m

4 Sedgeford to Holme next the Sea

through Ringstead (and Hunstanton)
6¼ miles (10.1 km), excluding Hunstanton option

If you have stopped at Sedgeford, return along Fring Road to rejoin the Peddars Way. At Fring Cross **12** the path curves up a stiff incline on the field headland on the east side of the hedge, which marks the line of the Peddars Way. The worst of the climb over, it passes Dovehill Wood and switches to the other side of the hedge. Follow the path to the corner of the field **A**.

Turn left, then right, and pass a line of cottages – the hamlet of Littleport – before emerging on the B1454 Sedgeford–Docking road. Cross the road, turn right, and after a short distance turn left into a drive leading to The Magazine Farm.

A short distance beyond The Magazine Farm, at the end of a grassy lane, the trail crosses the cinder trackbed of the old Heacham–Wells railway line. Cross over and follow the path to a T-junction; turn left and then right towards a distant shelter belt. Pass through the gap in the hedge **B**. The route turns slightly and skirts the edge of a tree belt.

Sedgeford Magazine is thought to have been built as a powder store or armoury in about 1640.

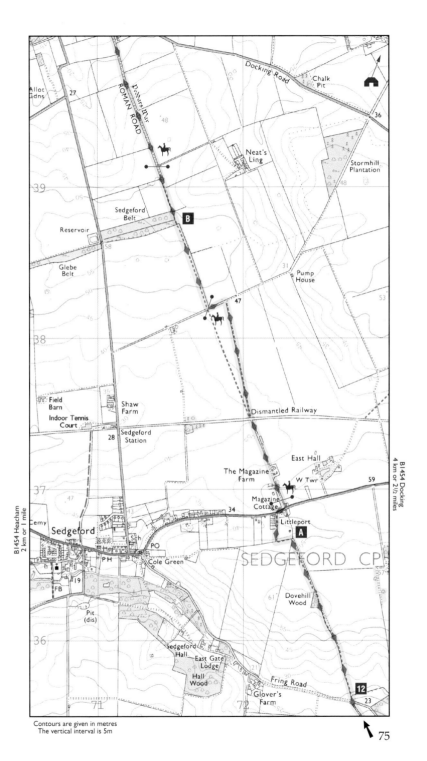

Contours are given in metres
The vertical interval is 5m

75

As Ringstead beckons, the Peddars Way begins to take on the look of a green lane. The Docking Road joins the route from the east, and shortly afterwards the trail turns left along a road, then right, and on through the village. Much of Ringstead is built of Norfolk carstone. Ringstead Downs nature reserve **13** (see page 80), a chalkland valley site, is a short distance away on the edge of the village.

On the far side of the village the trail turns right for a short distance, past a row of houses, and then turns left. It is possible that near here a branch of the Peddars Way once swung north-west towards Hunstanton. If you pause on the corner and look south across the fields, the line of the Way can be seen receding over the distant hills.

You are now about 2 miles (3 km) from the sea, and as the old windmill becomes an increasingly prominent landmark, so the Wash can sometimes be glimpsed to the west. Just beyond the row of houses, where a bungalow stands on its own, the route turns sharp left **C**. Green Bank, to the east, is thought to be of Iron Age origin.

Follow the headland path for about 400 yards (365 metres), then turn right. A line of bushes marks the way. This is probably the original line of the Roman road. Now the sea begins to dominate the view. Follow the field boundary between the bushes, which becomes a hedged, green lane, cross the Hunstanton road, and walk north along Seagate, a metalled road, towards the beach. The Roman terminus of the Peddars Way is not known – it simply peters out on the beach. Close by is the Holme Dunes nature reserve and Holme Bird Observatory **14** (see page 80), and the start of north Norfolk's famed maritime coast.

Holme is a popular spot with a fine beach and it was here, in 1986, that HRH the Prince of Wales declared the national trail open, watched by hundreds of spectators from amid the dunes.

A short distance before the beach is reached, a small bridge **D** over the River Hun marks the spot where the Peddars Way joins the Norfolk Coast Path.

If you wish to walk the 2½ miles (4 km) to Hunstanton (see page 83), turn left by the bridge and follow the path beside the caravans. Keep the Hun stream on your left and the golf links on your right. The path is well defined and easy to follow beside the fence. The outlines of Old Hunstanton soon appear and the track is pleasantly grassy.

14

Sluice

Flaxley

PC P

HOLME NEXT TH

D

Sprs

Caravan Park

Whitehall Farm

Caravan Park

Home Farm

FB

Littleholme

Seagate House

T

PH

War Meml

Nursery

Manor Farm

PO

Holme next the Sea

MS

Main Way

Manor House

Long Plantation

Wayside

Field Barn

Wind Pump

Wind Pump

The Pool

Half Moon Plantation

MS

Gipsy Green

North Belt

Green Bank

Birthday Wood

Hunstanton Hall Deodara Wood

Ozonea

C

Ilex Wood

stanton Park

Mill Farm

Kimberley Plantation

Windmill (disused)

The Stratch

ANTON CP

Green Broom Plantation

Holly Mount

Park Ho

Earthwork

Bluestone Farm

Gedding's Farm

Grove

Half Moon Plantation

War Meml Sch

Beech

PO

Ringstead

Carter's Plantation

Spring Meadow Pits

East End Farm

PH

Ringstead Bury

Glebe Farm

Burnham Road Fa

Docking Road

Field Barn

Elms

13

Hall Farm

Nature Reserve

St Peter's Church (remains of)

Ringstead Downs

Contours are given in metres
The vertical interval is 5m

A149 Hunstanton 2 km or 1 mile
Old Hunstanton

ON CP

A149 Thornham 2 km or 1 mile

Peddars Way & Norfolk Coast Path

Peddars Way

River Hun

Links Way & Norfolk Coast Path

Sedgeford Belt lines the horizon as the Peddars Way moves ever closer to Ringste

and the sea.

At the gate at the end of the links, follow Golf Course Road as it swings right. It takes you past the clubhouse and car park and along a lane. At the junction turn sharp right, walk down a cobbled road towards the beach, and turn left in front of the lifeboat shed. Take the sandy path on the bank at the rear of the beach huts and follow it until it emerges on to the grassy swathe of the car park on top of the cliffs. The Wash looms large, and the sea sweeps away towards the Lincolnshire coast. At the end of the car park turn left, away from the sea, and walk along Lighthouse Close, turning right into Cliff Parade. You will see the coastguard station, the old lighthouse, and the ruins of St Edmund's chapel. It was erected in 1272 to commemorate the AD 855 landing of Edmund, later King of East Anglia. Walk towards the town, passing Esplanade Gardens.

For walkers who have not followed Peddars Way thus far, but who would like to enjoy the Coast Path, Hunstanton **15** is a convenient starting point. Begin the walk on the central green and follow the path through the gardens past the café and on over a grassed area. Pass the old lighthouse, walk across the car park and find the sandy path leading along the back of the beach huts. Turn right by the lifeboat shed and then sharp left at the top of the lane. Follow the gravelled lane past the golf clubhouse and, where the lane bends right, go through the gate leading along the edge of the golf links near the little River Hun. Follow the path and the river along the edge of the course, past the caravans, and turn left at the bridge **D** (see map on page 77).

Ringstead Downs

A rare Norfolk example of chalk grassland, Ringstead Downs **13**, in the care of Norfolk Wildlife Trust (NWT), is a dry valley cut by glacial meltwaters. Plant life is particularly diverse on the south-facing slope, and includes rock rose, stemless thistle, salad burnet and wild thyme; this is also a good area for butterflies. The Downs look deceptively man-made, but they are not. The woods are out of bounds.

Holme Dunes National Nature Reserve

Holme Dunes is managed by Norfolk Wildlife Trust, and Holme Bird Observatory **14** is cared for by Norfolk Ornithologists' Association. The Bird Observatory is a 7-acre (2.8-hectare) plot of pines, scrub and grassland within the NWT reserve. There is a warden, hides and a nature trail. More than 285 bird species have been recorded.

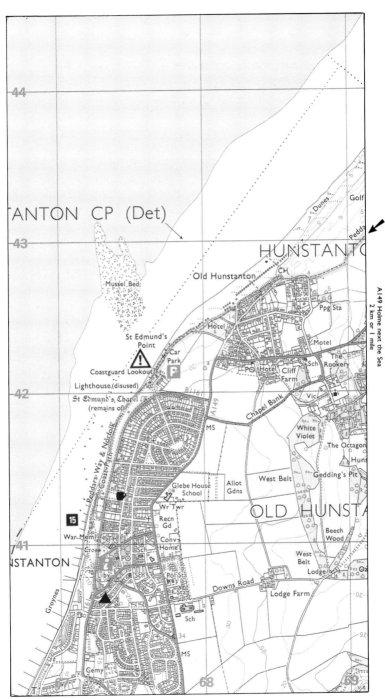

TANTON CP (Det)

HUNSTANTON

Old Hunstanton

CH

Mussel Bed

Dunes

Golf

Ppg Sta

St Edmund's
Point

Car
Park

Hotel

Motel

Coastguard Lookout

P

PO

Hotel

Cliff
Farm

Sch

The
Rookery

Lighthouse (disused)

St Edmund's Chapel
(remains of)

B 1161

A 149

Chapel Bank

Vic

MS

White
Violet

The Octagon

Peddars Way & Norfolk

Coast Path

Glebe House
School

Allot
Gdns

West Belt

Gedding's Pit

Huns

OLD HUNSTA

15

Wr Twr

Recn
Gd

Beech
Wood

War Meml

TH

Conv
Home

Cross

HUNSTANTON

Liby

i

PO

Sch

Sch

Pol Sta

F Sta

Downs Road

West
Belt

Lodge

Oa

Lodge Farm

Groynes

Sch

MS

Cemy

67

68

69

A 149 Holme next the Sea
2 km or 1 mile

Contours are given in metres
The vertical interval is 5m

Holme Dunes reserve is owned in part by the NWT and was established in 1965. It covers 550 acres (223 hectares) between the village and Thornham channel, and includes extensive sand and mud flats, dunes, saltmarshes, freshwater and brackish marshes, and grazing land.

The area is rich in insect and plant life, including marsh orchid, shrubby sea-blite, sea lavenders, and many species of moth and butterfly. In winter, bird-watchers enjoy seeing bunting and brent geese and enormous flocks of shore waders; in spring the area is famous for the passage of migrant warblers and chats; while autumn is fine for waders such as greenshank, green sandpiper, passerines and sea birds. Rarities are a speciality. During the Second World War the area was used as an artillery range.

Maritime matters

Maritime trade has had a profound effect on the Norfolk coastline, but the east coast has always been dangerous. At the beginning of the twentieth century there were 27 Royal National Lifeboat Institution stations between Hunstanton and Aldeburgh, in Suffolk. Disasters haunt these shores. There was the terrible gale of 1703, with enormous loss of life and shipping. Again, at the beginning of the twentieth century, 500 vessels are known to have been lost, stranded or wrecked in a three-year period; while on 28th October 1882, 13 ships perished between Lowestoft and Covehithe.

Despite this, trade flourished. Yarmouth once had 2,000 fishing craft, and as long ago as 1565 a state paper relating to customs and ports was able to mention – in addition to King's Lynn, the head port – Heacham, Hunstanton, Thornham, Burnham, Brancaster, Wells, Blakeney, Wiveton, Cley, Salthouse, Weybourne, Sheringham and Cromer. There are also records of local boats joining the fleet to oppose the Armada. But most of the trade was unromantic: timber, grain, oil cake, malt, coal, and boats going to or from the fishing grounds. It was drainage, silt and sand accretion, economics, and the coming of the railways that together squeezed most of the little ports dry.

Today, the north and north-west coastline of Norfolk is dotted with reminders of this remarkable past, glimpses of which can still be seen on Wells's quay, and in the shellfish boats of Brancaster and Burnham Overy Staithe and the crabbers of Sheringham and Cromer.

Hunstanton

The creation of 'new' Hunstanton **15** as an unusual west-facing resort was begun by Henry le Strange, Lord of the Manor, in about 1846, and was considerably boosted by the arrival of the railway in 1862. It still has the genteel air of the late-Victorian seaside town, with large hotels and villas grouped around a sloping triangular green. Beach houses from the 1930s line cliff roads, which push out towards Old Hunstanton; but the core of the town, much of it built in the distinctive local carstone, remains the area around the green.

Badly damaged by floods in 1953, Hunstanton is defended partly by a substantial sea wall and partly by another major attraction, the famous but fast-eroding 60-foot (18-metre) striped cliffs comprising layers of white chalk, red limestone and carstone. Alas, the railway station and the pier (destroyed by a storm in 1978) have gone, but modern facilities include leisure and sea life centres. There are gardens and a theatre, a fine beach, and when wind and weather permit, the coast of Lincolnshire – including Boston's famous church, The Stump – can be glimpsed on the other side of the Wash. Hunstanton is popular with boating and water-ski enthusiasts, and short sea trips are even possible to see the Wash seals.

Hunstanton's unusual 'striped' cliffs are a distinctive feature of this west-facing resort.

The sea thunders in the distance in this close-up view of Holme Dunes not far

rom Gore Point.

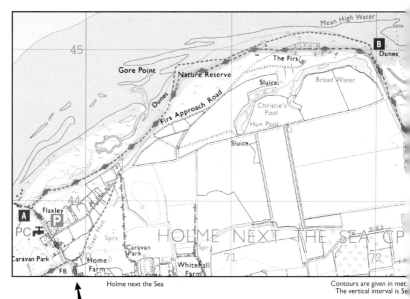

Holme next the Sea

Contours are given in met
The vertical interval is 5

5 Holme next the Sea to Burnham Overy Staithe

via Thornham and Brancaster
13¾ miles (22 km)

Holme next the Sea is a neat village of narrow lanes, but Beach Road can become impossibly crowded at peak periods.

Walk past the golf links towards the dunes and turn right **A** on to the sandy path leading to the nature reserve. It runs beside pools and the lavender marsh, and becomes increasingly lonely as it continues towards the sandy headland of Gore Point. The waymarked trail follows an impressively long boardwalk that dips and rolls through the nature reserve. An alternative is to walk by the beach. Either way, do not trample on the dunes. Black fragments scattered on the beach are the remains of the ancient forest of the North Sea basin, now reduced to clumps of a wet peaty substance.

The boardwalk gives way to a conifer plantation, and shortly afterwards the trail swings right **B** near the tip of Broad Water to join a sea defence bank. There are good views of the coastline (see page 92) and of the channel leading to the old harbour of Thornham (see page 92). Stay on the bank as far as the site of an old windmill, then turn left **C** along an uneven path and right into the village.

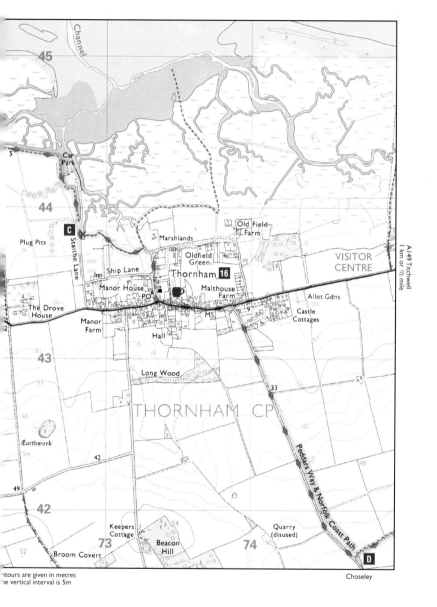

Contours are given in metres
The vertical interval is 5m

Choseley

Follow the main road through Thornham village **16**. There is no safe seaward route east towards Titchwell **17** (see page 94), so the trail makes a brief inland incursion. Turn right on the lane signposted to Choseley. There is now a tedious $1\frac{1}{4}$-mile (2-km) uphill trudge through an increasingly lonely landscape. At the triangular plantation turn left **D** and follow

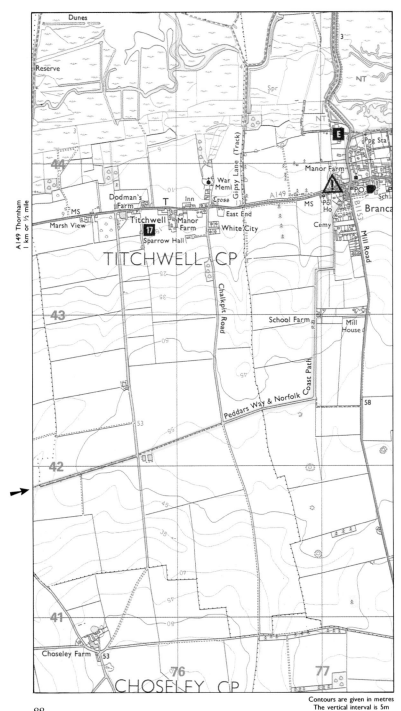

Contours are given in metres
The vertical interval is 5m

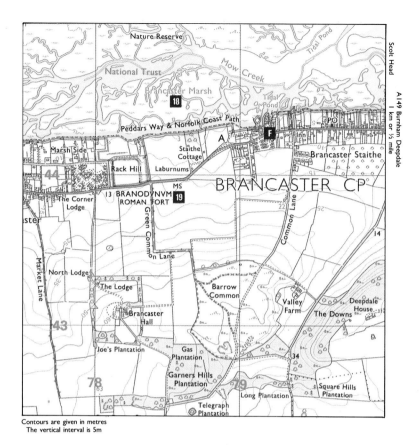

Contours are given in metres
The vertical interval is 5m

the hedge along a field headland and then on to a green
path. There is some good walking before the route turns
towards the coast and approaches Brancaster along a country
lane.

Cross over the main road and walk by St Mary's Church
towards the beach, as far as a National Trust sign, and turn
right **E**. On the edge of Brancaster Marsh **18** a boardwalk has
been laid which passes Rack Hill and the Roman site of
Branodunum **19** (see page 94), and shortly after a stile the route
turns left **F** behind some houses. Walk past the Staithe yacht
club and through the gap between some fishermen's sheds.

Brancaster Staithe once had a regular sea trade in coal and
grain, and what is believed to have been one of the largest
malthouses in the country. Hemmed in by saltings, it is still
a popular sailing centre. A ferry runs to Scolt Head **20** (see
page 96).

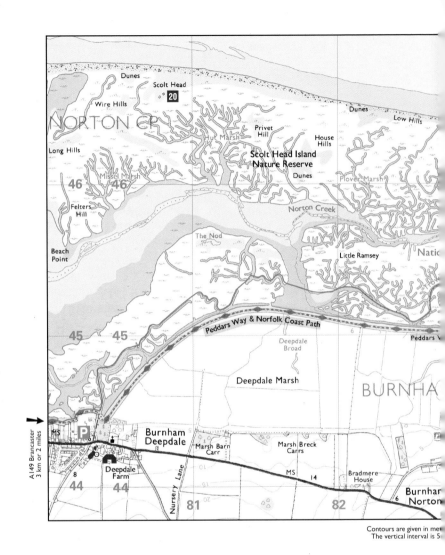

Contours are given in me
The vertical interval is 5

The trail runs along the top of the sea bank, but it is soon possible to pick up a lower, seaward path. Use either, according to whim or conditions. You may be able to see something of the local shellfish industry. Shellfish were brought ashore on this coast in Roman times. Today, fishermen collect young mussels ('seed') from breeding grounds in the Wash and leave them to grow in 'lays' in the creeks. Once grown, they are sorted and washed in cleansing pools.

This is also 'Nelson country' (see page 96) and from Burnham Deepdale you follow the wide sweep of the sea bank,

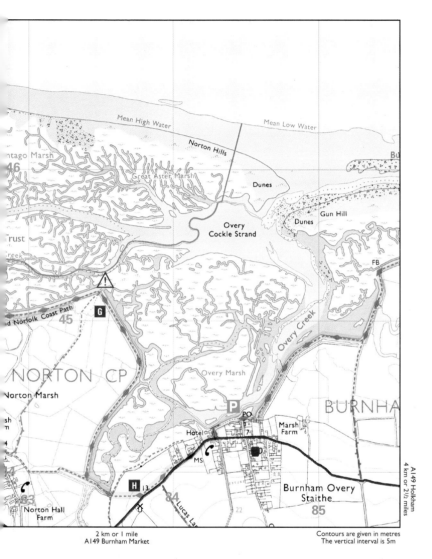

2 km or I mile
A149 Burnham Market

A149 Holkham
4 km or 2½ miles

Contours are given in metres
The vertical interval is 5m

which stretches towards Scolt Head **20** and Gun Hill. It is a
marvellous world of birds and creeks, wind and sky. At **G** take
care not to walk straight on to the marsh, but follow the bank
where it swings right. A disused windmill, used for holiday
accommodation, looms over the skyline ahead. Turn left over
the tiny River Burn on a cross bank and follow the trail across
the middle of a field, where it finally turns left **H** and runs
parallel with the A149 road into Burnham Overy Staithe. Walk
into the village and turn left towards the quay.

91

A fragile coastline

North Norfolk boasts one of the most unspoilt coastlines in England, and natural physical processes have developed it as a series of shingle ridges, sand flats, dunes and spits. Enclosed areas have become fresh marshes and grazing land, while others remain as saltings and brackish marshes. The variations in habitats and the natural processes are a delight to specialist and naturalist alike. Largely because of this scientific importance there is now an unbroken series of nature reserves from Holme to Weybourne, which are owned or administered by the National Trust, the Norfolk Wildlife Trust, the Royal Society for the Protection of Birds and English Nature.

In a sense, what you see today is merely a snapshot, because the influences of tide, weather and a host of other factors will have created different shapes tomorrow. Many of yesterday's ports, for example, are today becoming increasingly landlocked as silt accretion throttles outlets to the sea. So it is a fragile landscape. A constant threat of flooding and the effects of erosion represent one prong of the attack. Huge numbers of visitors represent another. Traffic development and visitors all threaten the special character of the area. In an effort to protect this character, the Norfolk Coast Project has produced a management strategy aimed at balancing the seemingly opposing demands of recreation and development. If this strategy is to be successful visitors will need to embrace the code of conduct printed at the back of this guide.

Thornham

This is transitional country between carstone and flint, and Thornham **16** has examples of both. It also has three large pubs. Shallow-draught boats plied their trade along this wind-swept coast in medieval times, and the harbour's capacity was increased in the 17th century when the River Hun was diverted to Thornham to enable the marshes to be drained. Granaries, jetties and a barn carried on a trade in oil cake, coal, timber, malt and farm produce. Then the railways began to siphon off the business and the harbour died. The last granary was demolished by floods in 1953. In 1887, as sea trade diminished, Thornham turned its attention to ornamental iron-working, and by 1899 smiths were turning out inn signs, fire screens and railings. The forges declined during the First World War, and closed in 1920.

Fishing boats and still waters in Thornham Channel in the early morning, with the sun about to break through the clouds.

Titchwell

Sea walls were built at Titchwell **17** in the 1780s and the marsh reclaimed for agricultural use, but the tidal surge of 1953 destroyed the defences. The fields reverted to saltmarsh. During the Second World War the area was used as a tank firing range, but in 1973 the Royal Society for the Protection of Birds bought 420 acres (170 hectares) and a few years later leased the foreshore. The habitat includes tidal and freshwater reed beds, salt and freshwater marsh, sand dunes and shingle beach, a section of which is sometimes roped off to protect nesting birds. The reserve is rich in habitats – in summer the saltmarsh is a profusion of sea lavender and sea aster – and in bird species: little tern, reed warblers, moorhen, marsh and hen harriers, bittern, brent geese, finches, twites, mallard, plover, dunlin, avocets and oystercatchers among others, depending on the time of year. There is a visitor centre.

Branodunum

The calm of Roman Norfolk began to be disturbed towards the end of the 2nd century A D when Angles, Saxons and Frisians from northern Germany and Holland began to harry the coast. In Britain, the Roman response was to develop a defensive framework in which the army and fleet worked together, and the building of coastal garrison forts from Norfolk to Hampshire. These were under the command of a new military supremo, the Count of the Saxon Shore.

Excavations at Branodunum **19** revealed substantial buildings inside the fort – which had stone walls 11 feet (3.3 metres) thick, backed by ramparts and a ditch – and extensive settlement areas nearby. The fort seems to have been occupied throughout the 4th century, and the first garrison may have been the 1st Cohort of Aquitanians, later replaced by a cavalry regiment, the Equites Dalmatae, from Dalmatia in northern Yugoslavia.

The forts – there were others at Burgh Castle and Caister on Sea, near Great Yarmouth, and possibly a fourth in the vicinity of Cromer – may have been linked by signal stations, for hills at the edge of marshes, including Gramborough Hill at Salthouse, Muckleburgh Hill at Kelling and Warborough Hill at Stiffkey, all have Roman sites on top. Stone robbing in the 18th century and subsequent agricultural operations removed most visible traces of Branodunum.

Brancaster

Branodunum shore fort is cared for by the National Trust, but it is only a part of the Trust's 2,150-acre (870-hectare) holding at Brancaster. The land also includes 4½ miles (7.2 km) of tidal foreshore, beach, sand dunes and saltings opposite Scolt Head island. There are strict limitations on car parking. The public is asked to keep off the sand banks and saltmarsh, so some of the best views are from the trail boardwalk.

Mussels brought from creeks are sorted and cleaned in the cleansing pools of Brancaster Staithe.

Scolt Head

The 1,620 acres (656 hectares) of dune, marsh and shingle ridge that comprise Scolt Head island are owned jointly by the National Trust and Norfolk Wildlife Trust, and leased to English Nature. It has been a nature reserve since 1923. The island supports a variety of marine flora – including glasswort, sea aster, thrift and sea lavender – and animal life, and is noted for its large colonies of nesting sandwich terns. Oystercatchers and many other species of wading birds are much in evidence while, out to sea, kittiwakes, gannets and arctic skuas can also be regularly seen. There is also a nature trail.

Nelson country

It is said there were once seven Burnham villages, though only five properly survive: Deepdale (its Saxon round-tower church has a marvellous Norman font), Norton, Market, Overy and Thorpe. In some old documents the Burnhams collectively were considered a port, but as boats became larger and trains appeared, the tortuous channels were less of a commercial proposition. The area oozes reminiscences of the sea, most obviously the pubs: The Nelson, The Victory, The Trafalgar, The Norfolk Hero, even simply The Hero. Burnham Market has the Hoste Arms, named after a famous naval commander. Captain Richard Woodget, Master of the *Cutty Sark*, lived at Overy and is buried in Burnham Norton churchyard. And the village of Cockthorpe was the birthplace, in 1650, of 'Norfolk's other Nelson', Sir Cloudesley Shovel, who distinguished himself in a string of actions. Returning from the siege of Toulon, Shovel's ship ran aground among the Scilly Isles. A woman found him semi-conscious on the beach, strangled him, and took his ring. Sir Cloudesley lies buried in Westminster Abbey.

England's most famous seaman, and Norfolk's local hero, Horatio Nelson, was born at Burnham Thorpe in 1758. His father, the rector, sent him to school in Norwich and North Walsham, and in 1771 he joined HMS *Raisonable*. Seven years later he returned to Burnham Thorpe with his wife, Fanny, to live quietly. In 1793, however, he was appointed captain of the *Agamemnon*, and by the time he landed at Great Yarmouth in 1800, with Sir William and Lady Hamilton, and following a host of daring escapades, he was a hero. A decade after his death his daughter, Horatia, returned to Burnham Market to stay with Nelson's sister, and later married the curate there.

A CIRCULAR WALK AT BRANCASTER

5¼ miles (8.4 km) approx.

This walk offers a delightful contrast between coast and country. Begin at the layby next to Burnham Deepdale church. With its round tower, Norman font and medieval glass, it is well worth a look. From the church, cross the road and turn right along it to the junction, where you turn left into a narrow, metalled lane. This passes through a sheltered and wooded valley until it reaches a junction amid the trees. Follow the lane to the right, and at the T-junction walk across and bear right on to Barrow Common. The common is thick with bracken and gorse bushes, but the path finally emerges on the far side of the common, crests a rise, and offers a marvellous panorama of sea and coast.

Follow Green Common Lane to the main road and turn left on to a path beside the road. You can see the Roman site of Branodunum **19**. Cross the road, turning right, and walk the narrow streets of Brancaster, before the route emerges on to the Coast Path boardwalk, which runs past Rack Hill. Follow the waymarks by Brancaster Staithe, Dial House and the sailing club. Turn right, back to the layby, at the point where the Coast Path swings left on to the sea bank. This walk will take you about 2¼ hours.

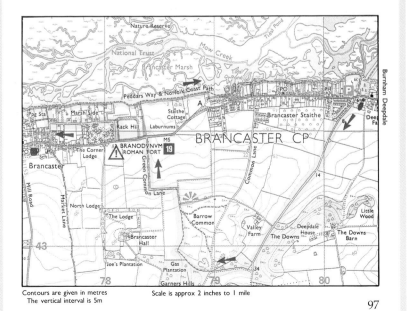

Contours are given in metres
The vertical interval is 5m

Scale is approx 2 inches to 1 mile

Overy mill beckons in the distance across the wide expanse of Burnham Norton Marsh.

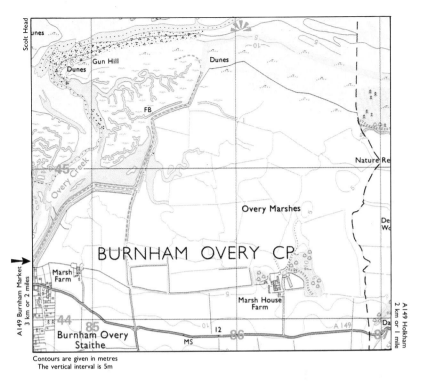

Contours are given in metres
The vertical interval is 5m

6 Burnham Overy Staithe to Stiffkey

past Holkham Bay and through Wells-next-the-Sea
10½ miles (16.9 km)

Burnham Overy Staithe – not to be confused with the smaller Burnham Overy Town, which may have preceded it as a port – clings to the A149 coast road but seems reluctant to turn its back on the sea. Granaries and maltings flourished here for as long as the barges, schooners and brigs could ply their trade. Even now the village is a favourite place for sailors, and the waters of Overy Creek and Overy Cockle Strand are invariably dotted with sails. Bright coloured waterproofs, naval caps and the slap of stays on metal masts are everyday sights and sounds.

Once on the sea bank there is some good, airy walking, flanked on one side by the foreshore and saltings, and on the other by reclaimed grazing and arable marshes, which huddle behind protective banks. The dunes loom large, and there are seaward views towards Scolt Head **20**.

99

Gun Hill is a surprisingly large barrier. The dunes are high and sometimes very hot. It is said that in summer the temperature here can rise to above 86°F (30°C). Make your way on to the beach – stay on existing tracks, to minimise damage – but keep clear of fenced areas, which in May, June and July protect colonies of nesting terns.

A marvellous vista opens up. Holkham Bay (see page 106) is a national nature reserve, at more than 10,130 acres (4,100 hectares) the largest in England and Wales. From Gun Hill it stretches towards the distant skyline, and an expanse of sea and sand shimmers in the sun. It is about 2½ miles (4 km) to Lady Ann's Road. If the sand is dry and progress is difficult, then it is a good idea to look for slightly wetter and marginally firmer surfaces closer to the high-water line. It may bring partial relief to aching limbs.

The great sweep of the bay attracts thousands of visitors each year, and the car park can become very busy at peak periods; but such is the amount of space – sea, sand, and pine shelter-belts to landward, planted about 1860 to protect reclaimed land from windblown sand – that the bay rarely conveys an impression of being crowded. A short distance inland are the earthworks of what is thought to have been an Iron Age fort. In AD 47 a faction of the local Iceni tribes rebelled against the authority of Rome. The revolt was crushed, and the geographical description of the final battle handed down by the Roman historian Tacitus might be applied to this fort. Equally, it might have referred to another fort site in the Cambridgeshire fens. The fort can be seen from a bird hide at Burrow Gap. Holkham Hall and the famous Holkham estate are nearby.

Follow the curve of the bay towards Lady Ann's Road, which is the main access point to the beach and the car park. A boardwalk has been laid over sections of the dunes. At the end of the boardwalk turn left **A** on to the path behind the trees.

The path is sheltered and the smell of the pines, sandy surfaces and clumps of willowherb give it something of the air of Breckland. Trees and dunes shield any sea breeze, and in summer it can become quite hot.

In a sense the path is a tangible and useful link between the vast and empty expanse of the bay and the busier prospect of Wells, visible intermittently in the distance through the trees; a final period of peace and quiet before the hubbub of holiday trade and traffic begins to dominate the senses.

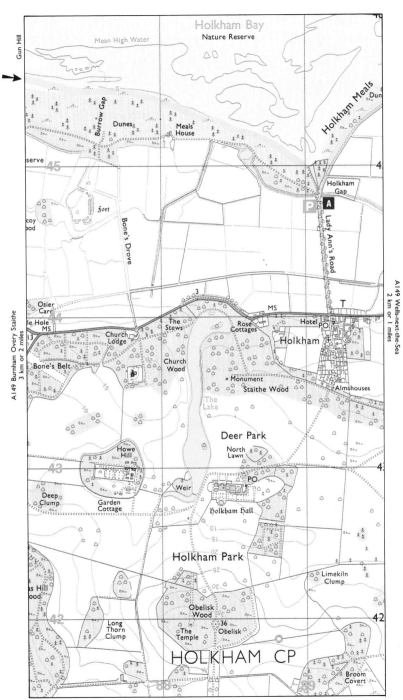

Gun Hill

Holkham Bay
Nature Reserve

Mean High Water

Burrow Gap

Dunes

Meals House

Holkham Meals

Dun

serve

45

Fort

coy ood

Bone's Drove

Holkham Gap

P A

Lady Ann's Road

A149 Wells-next-the-Sea
2 km or 1 miles

3

MS

T

Osier Carr

e Hole MS

The Stews

Rose Cottages

Hotel
PO

Holkham

Bone's Belt

Church Lodge

Church Wood

Monument

Staithe Wood

Almshouses

A149 Burnham Overy Staithe
3 km or 2 miles

The Lake

Deer Park

Howe Hill

North Lawn

43

Weir

PO

Deep Clump

Garden Cottage

Holkham Hall

Holkham Park

Limekiln Clump

s Hill ood

42

Long Thorn Clump

Obelisk Wood

The Temple

Obelisk

HOLKHAM CP

Broom Covert

Contours are given in metres
The vertical interval is 5m

101

Closer to Wells-next-the-Sea there are likely to be more strollers, for more paths strike off through the trees towards the beach. It is a popular place. And when the path finally emerges alongside Abraham's Bosom lake – now a boating lake and once a haven for fishing boats – the general appeal of the area becomes clear. There are camping and caravan sites and a car park. On top of the bank there is a good view of the lifeboat shed **21** and the great sweep of the beach, which, close to the trees, is fringed by beach huts. In summer it is thronged with visitors.

The trail runs along the top of the bank, beside the channel, but in summer it is also possible to use the narrow-gauge railway that runs beside Beach Road to reach the town of Wells-next-the-Sea **22** (see page 107). Despite problems of sea-going access through the narrow channel, this is now the only port on the north Norfolk coast with a usable harbour. The

Working boats and boys fishing – they all find a place along Wells quay.

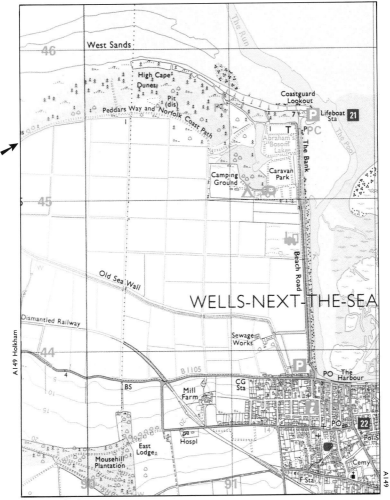

Contours are given in metres
The vertical interval is 5m

town and surrounding areas were badly damaged by floods in 1953, and in 1978 gales lifted a coaster out of the water and dumped it on the quay.

There is a great temptation to linger in Wells-next-the-Sea. It works hard at being a port, a busy town and a leisure centre. Along the main quay the smell of chips and the shouts of bingo callers mingle with the sight and sounds of children fishing for crabs. Souvenir shops jostle for attention, visitors gape, whelk boats prepare for sea, and residents go about their business. It is a fascinating mix.

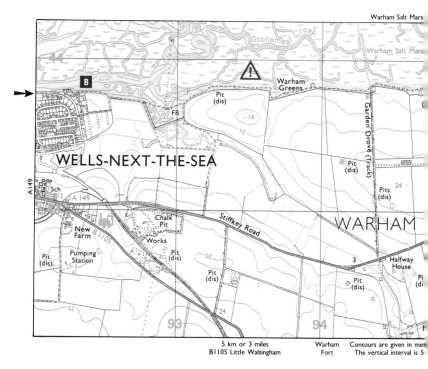

5 km or 3 miles
B1105 Little Walsingham

Warham
Fort

Contours are given in met
The vertical interval is 5

Walk along the quay past the boats and pubs, chandler and shops, to the end of East Quay **B**. Just beyond a slipway, where the road divides, turn slightly left and take the metalled road between the sheds, then left on to a footpath and up on to the bank. The town is quickly left behind, and saltmarshes begin to dominate the view again. After a time the bank turns right and then left, around the fringes of an inlet. Then it turns left again and plunges into dense undergrowth.

The path between the bushes is quite distinct and it emerges into open country on the edge of Warham saltmarshes. The path is springy and the walking comfortable, and the way eventually evolves into a broad, grassy swathe dominated to the north by marshes, birds and glimpses of the far-off sea. In July and August violet-blue sea lavender flowers tinge the brown creeks. Behind, the dark, pencil-slim lines of the Holkham and Wells tree-belts can still be seen on the horizon.

Do not, incidentally, be lured on to the marsh. There are occasional tantalising glimpses of seaward paths, but these are not recommended; first, because of the danger – the creeks and rivulets flood at high tide – and second, because of a need to protect the fragile marshes from the tramp of too many feet.

104

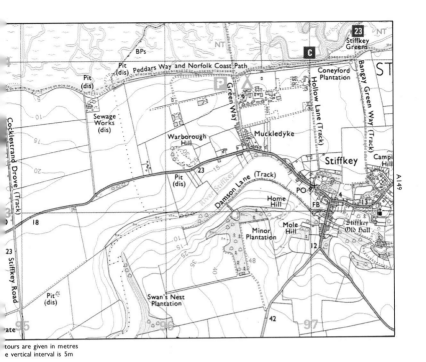

tours are given in metres
e vertical interval is 5m

Incidentally, about 2 miles (3.2 km) away at Warham is one of the most atmospheric sites in the whole of Norfolk. For many years Warham fort was thought of as 'Danish', but it seems more likely to have been constructed during the Iron Age, and was probably set against a background of a growing population and an increasingly wealthy aristocratic society. Whatever the dating, the massive ditches and ramparts enclose about $3\frac{1}{2}$ acres (1.4 hectares) on a slope above the River Stiffkey.

This is bracing walking, although if the breeze is off the land it can become quite warm. The remains of military hardwear begin to increase. Remnants of concrete footings and roads can be seen, testimony to the military importance of the area for defence or training throughout two world wars.

Beyond Green Way, by the car park, the path plunges on towards Bangay Green Way – one of a series of lanes and tracks that stretch like fingers from the coast road to the marshes – which can provide access to the village of Stiffkey. Stiffkey Greens and saltmarshes **23** dominate the seaward scene (see page 108).

If you want to stop in Stiffkey, leave the Coast Path at **C** and walk half a mile (1 km) into the village, along Hollow Lane.

Holkham

Holkham not only has a place in agricultural history, but the house, estate and bay are one of the county's top attractions. Indeed, the bay and the nature reserve lure 500,000 visitors a year. Holkham Hall attracts many thousands more. The figures underline the dilemma of reconciling the needs of the public with the needs of wildlife. Holkham reserve is managed by English Nature and includes foreshore, saltmarsh, pinewoods, scrub and dunes. Thousands of oystercatchers winter at Holkham, along with up to 8,000 knot, and the rare natterjack toad lives among the dunes. The reserve is open to the public.

The village and estate are synonymous with the name of Thomas Coke (pronounced Cook), 1752–1842. An MP and a Whig, he was one of the great 'improving landlords' of the 18th and early 19th centuries, who produced sheep pasture from the sandy soils of his estate, encouraged the use of the Norfolk four-course crop rotation, modernised his farms and experimented with new breeds of sheep, cattle and pigs. The somewhat sombre neo-Palladian hall was begun in 1734 by the agriculturalist's great-uncle, also Thomas, who employed William Kent to design the furnishings. The rooms are hung with fine paintings and tapestries, and the estate also boasts tea rooms, a museum, craft and pottery centre, and a garden centre.

Lifeboats

Special lifeboat days and visits to lifeboat stations are high on the popularity lists of resident and visitor alike. Nowadays the yellow air-sea rescue helicopters tend to steal many of the headlines, lifeguards patrol many of the beaches, and inshore inflatables prowl the edges of the tides to rescue tired swimmers and airbed sunbathers floating out to sea. But lifeboats remain the backbone of the rescue service. They were once more numerous than they are now. Blakeney, Brancaster and Hunstanton all had large boats at one time, whereas now the service is concentrated on Wells-next-the-Sea and Cromer, although Hunstanton and Sheringham have inshore lifeboats. Each has its own history of heroic rescues, losses and larger-than-life characters.

Norfolk Shipwreck Association had a lifeboat at Wells-next-the-Sea in 1830, but the Royal National Lifeboat Institution

(RNLI) took over in 1857, opening a lifeboat station in 1869. The first lifeboat was named the *Eliza Adams*, financed from the Penny Readings Fund. The most recent, a Mersey-class lifeboat that cost £360,000, was named by the Duchess of Kent in 1990. Sheringham's first boat, the *Augusta*, was launched in 1836. In 1894 she was replaced by another privately financed boat, the *Henry Ramey Upcher*, and this boat, now preserved, can still be seen in the old Lifeboat Shed at Sheringham. Cromer's history is dominated by the late Henry Blogg, who held the position of coxswain until 1947. During this time he was awarded the George Cross, the British Empire Medal, and three gold and four silver medals by the RNLI. In fact Cromer's history is even longer than this, for the Shipwreck Association established a lifeboat there prior to 1825.

Wells-next-the-Sea

Wells-next-the-Sea **22** still exports farm produce, but the view from the quay has changed considerably. The long Beach Road embankment was not built until the 19th century, prior to which the main channel used to meander among creeks to the west. In the early 1800s this was the chief port between King's Lynn and Yarmouth, so for decades it has been a bustling place of cargoes and ropemakers, sailmakers, carters and chandlers. The agricultural prosperity of the area provided further impetus. Then, in 1857, the Wells and Fakenham railway line was opened, and decline began. Wells quay today is busier than at any time since the end of the last war, and fishing boats and leisure craft still negotiate the tricky channel.

The oldest surviving houses seem to date from the early 17th century, and the town is shaped around an elongated grid of streets leading back from the coast road. There is a suspicion that the sea once came almost as far as the church, and that in the 16th century there was a harbour in the vicinity. Not far from the church is The Buttlands, an open space that may or may not have been the site of archery butts, but which is still used for carnivals and summer events.

A short distance along the Stiffkey road is the Wells and Walsingham Light Railway, the longest 10-inch-gauge railway in Britain. From spring to autumn it makes 8-mile (13-km) return journeys along the old Great Eastern Railway trackbed to Walsingham, a centre of modern pilgrimage to the Anglican and Roman Catholic shrines and an important monastic centre in the Middle Ages.

Stiffkey

The National Trust has charge of Stiffkey Greens **23**, comprising 487 acres (197 hectares) of saltmarsh and 2 miles (3.2 km) of coastline. Sea lavender and sea aster are widespread and the undisturbed marshes are winter feeding grounds for brent geese, wigeon and teal. Little and common tern breed on the shingle banks. The marshes are also the source of the Stewkey Blue cockles, mentioned in the 17th-century writings of Sir Thomas Browne, of Norwich, who went on to praise the lobsters and crabs of Sheringham and Cromer and the oysters of Burnham and Hunstanton. In 1994 a geological find by a Reading University team on the marshes – nodules of mud hardening into pieces of stone in a few years, rather than the thousands it usually takes – was seized upon by creationists as evidence that the world did not evolve over millions of years, but was created 6–10,000 years ago. Warham Marsh is part of the 9,700-acre (3,926-hectare) national nature reserve that stretches all the way from Burnham Overy Staithe to Stiffkey.

The flinty village of Stiffkey is famous for two things, its cockles and a former parson. The cockles, known as 'Stewkey Blues', used to be gathered by the women of the village, but the fishery began to decline in the 1950s. Incidentally, Stiffkey is generally pronounced Stiffkey; it is thought Stewkey means stumps, and probably refers to the marsh valley. As for the parson, he was the Revd Harold Davidson, who was involved in a famous 1930s scandal. Deprived of his living for spending too much time in Soho, Davidson became known as the 'prostitutes' parson'. He embarked on a campaign to clear his name, which involved appearing in music hall, sitting in a barrel on Blackpool's Golden Mile, and in a lion's cage at Skegness. He died after being mauled by a lion. Henry Williamson, author of *Tarka the Otter* and *Salar the Salmon*, also lived in Stiffkey during the Second World War and wrote of his experiences in *The Story of a Norfolk Farm*.

7 Stiffkey to Weybourne

through Blakeney and Cley next the Sea
11¾ miles (18.9 km)/11½ miles (18.4 km) via alternative route

From Stiffkey village, rejoin the Coast Path at **C**. Then (sometimes grassed, sometimes stony), the path heads urgently towards Morston, and Blakeney Point (see page 116) begins to dominate the northern horizon. Around Freshes Creek it takes to a bank, turns a corner and levels out again on Morston Greens.

These marshes are part of the domain of the National Trust, and there are often good populations of redshank, shelduck and brent geese, and a variety of saltmarsh flora. There are also fine views of the long sliver of sand and shingle of the Point, and on sailing days you can glimpse the boats in Morston Creek. Breezes bluster unchecked across the marsh. Then Blakeney church, with its unusual outline, begins to make its presence known.

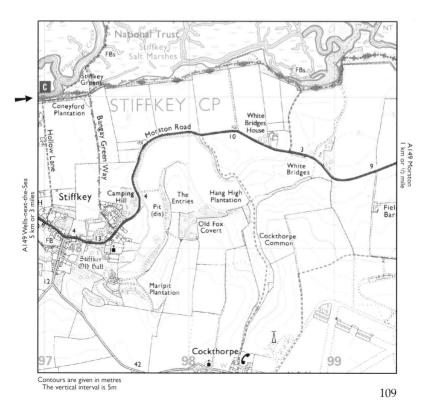

Contours are given in metres
The vertical interval is 5m

Contours are given in metres
The vertical interval is 5m

Morston village hides until the last moment, but it is a popular little place. Turn off the track into a narrow lane **A**, then left up some steps and across a car park. Walk past the many boats and on to the sea bank on the far side.

In summer the quay is invariably busy. A ferry runs to Blakeney Point, and that salty delicacy, samphire, can be found in the vicinity. Bait digging for lugworms is another local industry, as it is at Blakeney and Stiffkey.

Blakeney also tends to play hide-and-seek, for the grassy path on top of the bank zigzags haphazardly alongside Agar Creek. The masts of pleasure craft finally come into view. Then the path loops past Red House **B** and reaches the edge of the quay. Beside the quay is the channel, almost dry when the tide is out. About 1½ miles (2.4 km) inland of Blakeney, incidentally, are the Downs at Wiveton (see page 118).

In Blakeney, narrow streets of cobbled cottages lead down to the quay, and homes huddle together in yards. Even the bulky façade of the Blakeney Hotel, opened in 1923, sets a stubborn face against the wind. Nowadays the village is packed with people and pleasure craft in summer. It is also full of 'second homes' and is almost entirely reliant on tourism. In 1946, some of the old cottages were in such a squalid state that a housing trust was formed to begin a process of renovation. You can still see plaques on many of the buildings. And the village is fighting to retain its physical links with the sea, for the navigable creeks are silting up. Were a blockage to become permanent it would sever Blakeney from much of its history. This coast was once the 'gateway to England' for vast quantities of goods and

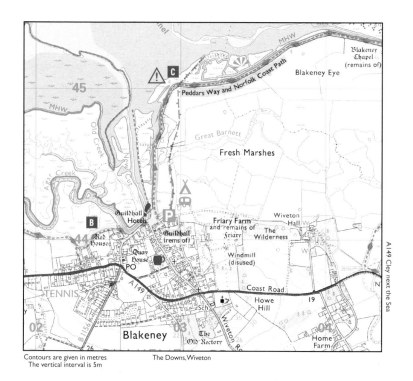

Contours are given in metres
The vertical interval is 5m

The Downs, Wiveton

cargoes, and the villages of Blakeney, Cley next the Sea and Wiveton all carry tell-tale signs of this former importance. In Blakeney it is most obviously seen in the 14th-century Guildhall. Blakeney boats were present at the siege of Calais in 1347, and by the 16th century its vessels were ranging as far as Iceland. When the Armada threatened, the three ports responded with a muster of 36 ships. The 15th-century church has a second, smaller tower at the north-east corner of the chancel. The main tower is a lofty landmark, so its smaller neighbour may have housed a beacon for shipping. A light is still kept burning there during the hours of darkness.

Walk the length of the quay, cross the car park and climb on to the sea bank. Now you face a marvellous 2¾-mile (4.4-km) walk along the top of the sea bank, as it curves out towards Blakeney Eye and inland again alongside Cley channel. The views are stunning, and on a breezy day with the hint of a storm in the offing there is a real feeling of isolation.

Two warnings. Do not try to cross the creeks to reach Blakeney Point; and take care at **C** and **D** (page 114) to stay on the main bank and do not stray along paths amid the creeks.

Cley's famous windmill peeps from behind a line of houses, which mark the edge

of the old channel.

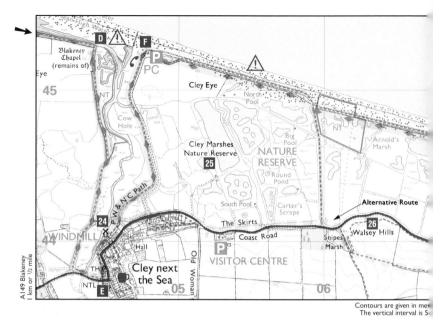

Contours are given in metres
The vertical interval is 5m

Cley next the Sea and its distinctive windmill slowly come into view. Beside the outline of the ruins of a 13th-century chapel (in the landward field, near **D**) the bank swings right and heads towards Cley. Along the shoreline to the east a rise in the ground indicates the rise of the cliffs beyond Weybourne.

Follow the bank to the Blakeney–Cley road, turn left and cross the sluice, then climb down from the bank by the steps **E**. Turn left into the village and left again down a narrow passage opposite a telephone box. Turn right at the end of the passage and follow the path by the quay wall to the mill **24**.

Cley next the Sea, once centred around its church, was a port from where wool from Norfolk sheep was shipped to the Low Countries. In the 13th century, Blakeney Haven (Cley, Blakeney and Wiveton) was one of the greatest ports in the country. But a bank built in the 17th century began to obstruct navigation to Wiveton and this, and marsh reclamation, finally forced Wiveton to cease trading as a port. In 1853, Cley's imposing Customs and Excise office also closed, and by 1855 the port was in serious decline. Even smuggling petered out. Today, Cley next the Sea is the nerve centre of the nation's 'twitchers' (birders who are constantly seeking new species), Cley Marshes **25** (see page 118) being one of the country's foremost bird reserves.

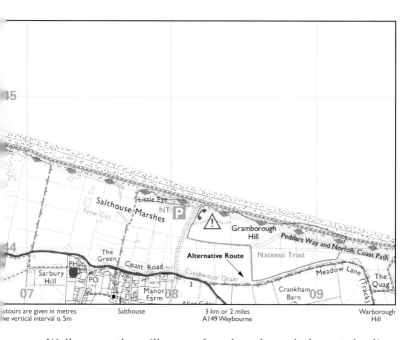

tours are given in metres
e vertical interval is 5m
Salthouse
3 km or 2 miles
A149 Weybourne
Warborough
Hill

Walk across the mill car park and go through the gate leading to a sea bank. Look out for an old war-time gun cupola. The path is uneven, and there are more steps. With raising sea levels, the shingle bank between Cley and Kelling is not sustainable, so the Environment Agency is allowing the coast here to retreat. A new clay sea-defence bank will be constructed along the line of the New Cut. The National Trail will be rerouted to follow a new line which will be developed over the period of the sea-defence construction, and may not be fully available until 2004. Where the Coast Path runs close to the Cley beach road, keep an eye out for signs directing you on to the new route. This is shown on the map as a broken yellow line. The old route, realigned to the top of the shingle, is still available as a public right of way.

The new route, while further from the sea, does have its compensations: a close encounter with the Cley National Nature Reserve and, nearer to Salthouse, stunning views over the whole of this stretch of coastline.

The curiously named Cley Eye, Little Eye, and Granborough and Sarbury Hills are hillocks, the first three much eroded by the sea. Some may also have been connected with the local salt-making industries, while others, on which Roman remains have been found, may have been used as signal stations. The new route passes by Walsey Hills **26** (see page 119). As you approach

115

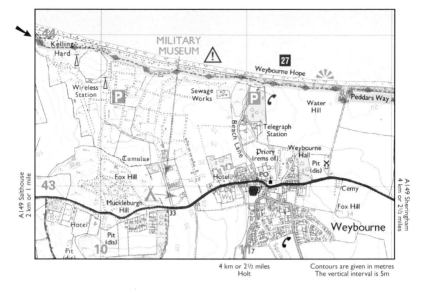

Weybourne Hope **27** (see page 119), the wire fences and buildings of a Ministry of Defence installation dominate the landward view. In 1993 an observatory to measure levels of air pollution was opened nearby.

Weybourne's windswept beach is often dotted with sea anglers enjoying the wild, crashing surf.

Blakeney Point

Blakeney Point is an elongated shingle spit. Dunes have been formed by windblown sand, and this has stabilised the vegetation. The 1,184-acre (479-hectare) area was acquired in 1912 and given to the National Trust to become the first reserve in Norfolk. It is of great interest to geographers and botanists, and is one of Britain's most important nesting sites for terns and other shore-nesting birds. In spring and autumn many migrant and rare species visit the Point, and in winter the harbour is the haunt of brent geese, ducks and waders. There is a colony of common and grey seals on the sand spits. Three distinct habitats – shingle, dune and marsh – support a rich tapestry of plant life, including sea rocket and sea campion, thrift and bird's-foot trefoil. The reserve is managed by a warden. It is open to the public and can be reached from Cley beach (a 6-mile (9.6-km) return walk along the shingle) or more easily by ferry from Blakeney or Morston quays.

116

Anglers at Weybourne beach are vividly outlined by the setting sun against a placid sea.

Wiveton Downs

This 17-acre (6.9-hectare) picnic site is a showpiece for anyone interested in Ice Age formations and deposits. There is a car park and footpaths, and the views are impressive. The site is actually the southern fringe of a ridge of sand and gravel, and it has helped geologists chart the limits of ice movement and discover more about landforms left by the departing ice. There is gorse and bracken and a number of different plant habitats.

Cley Marshes

In the 16th century, Cley Marshes **25** were covered by the sea at spring tides, and a navigable channel connected Salthouse with Cley harbour and Blakeney estuary. Subsequently the shingle beach has been moving landwards by about 3 feet (92 cm) a year and much of the original marshland, and the Salthouse channel, is now under the sea. In 1926, the marshes were purchased to provide a bird sanctuary, and Norfolk Naturalists' Trust (now the NWT) was formed to administer it. It was the first county naturalists' trust in Britain.

It is an exceptional site for rare birds and huge numbers of migrating waders and summer visitors, including spoonbill, black-tailed godwit and ruff. Avocet, bittern and common tern nest, and several thousand brent geese and wigeon, with

Cley Marshes – now a popular bird sanctuary attracting numerous visitors – seen from the bird-watchers' hide.

pintail, teal, mallard, shoveller, snow bunting and harrier, are among the winter visitors. The path along East Bank has been called 'the most famous bird walk in Britain'. A hint of a rarity brings enthusiasts flocking from all parts of the country, and there are a number of observation hides. Visitor and car parking permits can be obtained from the Dick Bagnell-Oakeley Centre on the main coast road between Cley and Salthouse. The reserve has been designated a European Community 'Special Area of Conservation'. Arnold's Marsh is owned by the National Trust and managed by the NWT. At Gramborough Hill, 68 acres (27.5 hectares) of marsh and seashore are owned by the National Trust and leased to the NWT.

Walsey Hills

Walsey Hills is a small reserve **26** comprising a gorse-covered hill and blackthorn thicket. It is just south of Cley's East Bank and adjoins the A149 coast road.

Weybourne Hope

The old rhyme goes, 'He who would old England win, must at Weybourne Hoop begin', but its origins are lost. Military associations with Weybourne Hope **27** go back centuries. The Hope, or Hoop, enables deep-draught boats to anchor close inshore, which bred one invasion scare after another. Elaborate defences were planned by Elizabeth I to meet the threat of invasion by Spain, and there was a military presence here during both world wars. During the First World War it was used as an embarkation point for troops leaving for France, during the Second World War gunnery ranges spawned emplacements and Army camps, while more recently mobile radar tracking units have been based here. There are also many stories of wrecks and smugglers.

In 1858, an undersea telegraph cable from Borkum, in Germany, was brought ashore here, and in 1950 a cable link with Esbjerg, in Denmark, was opened. The telegraph station is now shut. The steeply shelving beach is popular with beach anglers. Nearby is the Muckleburgh Military Collection, one of the largest private displays of tanks, armoured cars, guns and Army vehicles in the UK.

A circular walk at Blakeney

5¼ miles (8.4 km)

This is a walk round part of the area's maritime history. Park at Blakeney quay and begin walking along the sea bank. On the right are drained marshes, grazed by cattle, and on the left salt-marshes intersected by tidal creeks. Stay on the sea bank and turn right at the end of the barbed wire at Blakeney Eye. Follow the grassy path, which seems to head straight for Cley next the Sea. Just short of the coast road the bank turns left and the path crosses the sluice and goes on to the road down the

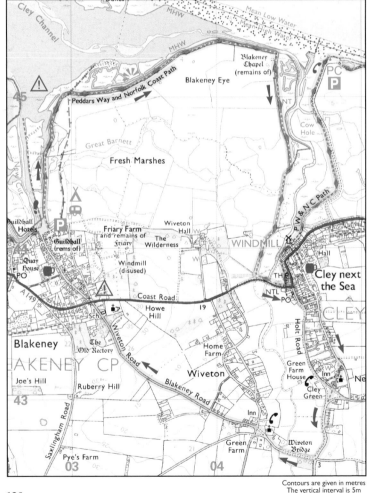

Contours are given in metres
The vertical interval is 5m

Pleasure craft line the quay at Blakeney, which is a popular place all year round.

steps. Turn right in the village, then first left, then right again. At the top of the gradient, near a house called The Knoll, turn into the leafy lane that dips towards the churchyard. Walk by St Margaret's church to the main gate.

This is Cley Green, site of the former port. Walk across the Green and take the Wiveton road. Wiveton church is now ahead and slightly to the right. Turn right and cross the medieval bridge. Again, this was once a bustling quayside. From the church, follow the signs to Blakeney. The road grinds uphill and is finally swallowed by trees on the outskirts of Blakeney. Pass the church, cross over the road, and take the narrow street signposted Blakeney Quay. A number of flint-faced homes and walls carry the plaque of the Blakeney Housing Association. This walk will take you about 2 hours. It is hoped that the section between Wiveton and Blakeney will eventually be extended to include Wiveton Downs.

8 Weybourne to Cromer

through Sheringham
8 miles (12.9 km)

At Weybourne Hope the shingle relents and the cliffs take over. Slowly at first, the path heads up the incline and skirts the edges, opening out the view. Clear days offer vistas of a shoreline curving towards the horizon and glimpses of far-off ships in Yarmouth Roads, or fishermen tending crab pots. Sea birds wheel and dive, and far below the surf crashes on to the beach. The cliffs are in a constant state of erosion, so resist the temptation to peer down the tumbling slopes.

There is a good illustration of this at Water Hill **A**, where the path turns sharply inland to skirt a line of houses. Not many years ago the path was on the seaward side; now, alas, it has gone over the edge. In 1994 a spectacular ravine, 100 yards

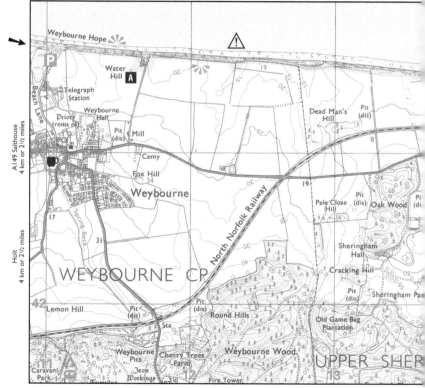

Contours are given in metre
The vertical interval is 5m

(92 metres) long and 15 feet (4.5 metres) deep, was carved out by surface water draining into the sea. Walkers must carefully skirt the ravine to regain the cliff path.

Inland, the views are equally fine. Much of this land is cared for by the National Trust. Sheringham Park, inland of Dead Man's Hill with access from the cliff path, has more than 700 acres (280 hectares). A tell-tale puff of smoke is also an indication of the closeness of North Norfolk Railway's Poppyland Line, a preserved steam railway running on the old Midland Great Northern track from Sheringham to Holt. Even the cliffs in this area – the so-called Cromer Forest Bed (see page 130) – are internationally famous.

Continue past the golf links and climb Skelding Hill to the old coastguard lookout. Walk down into Sheringham **28** (see page 130). Pass the boating pond and descend the slopes **B** to the promenade. Pass the old lifeboat house and walk along the upper prom to a toilet block at the far end **C**. Turn right

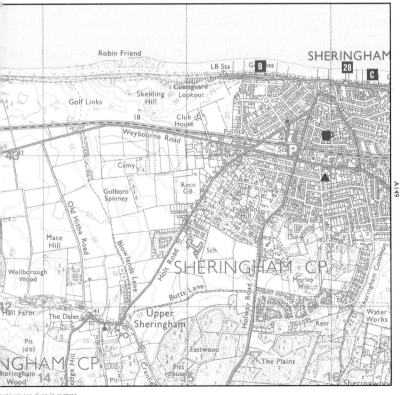

Contours are given in metres
The vertical interval is 5m

Looking west along Sheringham cliffs, the coastline curves towards Weybourne

and beyond.

and climb the steep steps up the hill. Carry on up the concrete slope, turn left by the putting green, and follow the path to the top of Beeston Hill **29**.

A pause by the Ordnance Survey triangulation point affords some magnificent views. Ahead are the villages of East and West Runton and, behind them, Cromer.

Descend Beeston Hill by the sandy steps and follow the path towards a caravan site. Turn right **D** by the hedge. Cross the railway line and then the main coast road. Not far away are the ruins of the 13th-century priory of St Mary in the Meadow. After first turning left along the old road, turn right on to a gravelled track leading towards Beeston Hall and follow the lane to the edge of the National Trust's property at The Roman Camp **30** (see page 130). In this area there are birch trees and bracken in evidence, and a smell of pine permeates the glades.

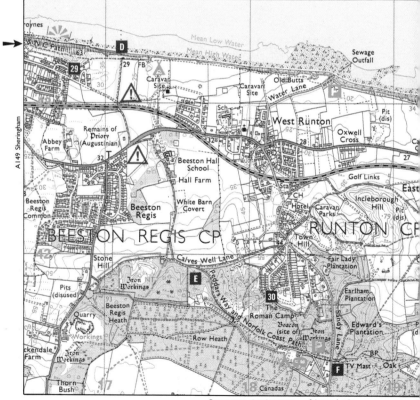

Contours are given in metres
The vertical interval is 5m

2 km or 1 mile
Felbrigg Hall

Walk a short distance along Calves Well Lane and turn right **E** into the trees. Follow the sandy uphill track all the way past the caravan site. There are occasional glimpses of the sea, and a nearby flagpole claims the highest elevation in Norfolk: 346 feet (105 metres).

Cross over Sandy Lane **F** and take the downhill track under the trees signposted to the left. At the camp site entrance continue right along the path beside the fields to reach a small common. From the common, a narrow, enclosed path leads east to Manor Farm. Pass under the cavernous arch of the loop line that connected the M&GN (Midland and Great Northern) Railway with the Great Eastern Railway from Norwich – the curving arch is a masterpiece of the bricklayer's art – and follow the trail towards Cromer. Felbrigg Hall (see page 132) is situated a few miles to the south, and there are increasing glimpses of Cromer church. When the path reaches a metalled road, and subsequently a main road, turn left and walk by the railway station.

There is no obvious end to the walk in Cromer **31** (see page 132) but there is an information board at the car park near the putting green. A nicer ending, it seems to me, is the sea front in sight of the pier and the shining sea. A beer and a crab sandwich will add immeasurably to a sense of achievement.

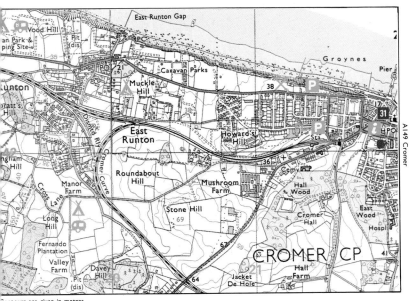

Contours are given in metres
The vertical interval is 5m

Sheringham beckons as the trail descends from the cliffs and prepares to enter its

final phase.

129

Cromer Forest Bed

Freshwater deposits of the Cromer Forest Bed are of great geological importance. The pebbles and shingle emanate from three sources – flints laid by ancient warm seas, glacial deposits, and deposits formed in the delta of a river, possibly the Rhine. In fact, the geological series appears intermittently in cliffs all the way from Weybourne to Kessingland, and plants such as oak, ash, hazel, lime, hornbeam, alder and pine have been identified. The bones and teeth of hippopotamus, hyena, deer and the Etruscan rhinoceros have also been found. More recently, and with help from National Lottery funding, the fossil bones of a huge 600,000-year-old elephant have been dug out of the cliffs between the Runton villages. Norwich Castle Museum has a special display.

Sheringham

Local fishermen still set their crab pots, as they have done for generations, for Sheringham **28** was a fishing village long before it became a railway-age boom resort. The leisure explosion came in the late 19th century, when much of the present town was built, but many of the old flint cottages, some now converted into shops, remain.

Today, it is a gritty town, full of Victorian and Edwardian houses, holiday trade and local industry. Sheringham is known for lobsters, crabs, whelks, a famous lifeboat station and for family nicknames – common in fishing communities – such as Downtide, Joyful and Paris. True locals are known as Shannocks, thought to derive from the dialect word shanny, meaning unruly; the word probably originated during periods of rivalry with the crabbers of Cromer.

The Roman Camp

The National Trust bought the 72-acre (29-hectare) Roman Camp **30** in the 1920s and acquired an additional 37 acres (15 hectares) of heath in 1970, but the name cannot be traced any further back than the early part of the twentieth century. It may derive from the site of a coastal beacon or telegraph station, possibly during the 14th to 17th centuries, or from a misinterpretation of a series of pits identified as evidence of Saxon-Norman-medieval iron smelting. It is a popular area for strolling – sandy paths dip and rise among glades. The trees include oak, ash, chestnut, beech, rowan, silver birch and Scots pine, and the area attracts large numbers of woodland birds.

Pale autumn sunshine filters through the trees across the leaf-strewn track at Beacon Hill.

Felbrigg Hall

Felbrigg is one of the finest 17th-century houses in Norfolk, with original 18th-century furniture and pictures. There is a traditional walled garden, recently restored by the National Trust as a decorative kitchen garden, an orangery with camellias, a large park, and lakeside and woodland walks. It was the home of the Windham family for 300 years.

Cromer

Labelled the Gem of the North Norfolk coast, Cromer **31** has been a popular resort for years. Already well known in the late 18th century, its development began in the 1890s with the opening of rail services to London and the Midlands. In 1883, Clement Scott, a London theatre critic, wrote an article in the *Daily Telegraph* extolling the quiet and colourful virtues of what subsequently became known as Poppyland. The locality became the gathering place of writers and poets, and a Poppyland 'industry' developed. The pier and many of the large hotels date from this period, lending an Edwardian atmosphere to yet another coastal community that tries to cope with the requirements of today.

Cromer has a dominating church with the tallest (160-foot/49-metre) parish tower in Norfolk, crab boats, a lovely beach, fishermen's cottages, shops selling crabs, narrow streets, deck chairs, beach huts, a pier and theatre, and even a lighthouse, now fully automatic. And it has its lifeboat station. Cromer was a front-line station during the Second World War, when its two boats were credited with the rescue of 450 people. Britain's most famous lifeboatman, the late Henry Blogg, was coxswain for more than 50 years and was the most decorated of them all. He received the RNLI gold medal three times, the silver medal four times, the George Cross and the British Empire Medal. He and his crews saved 873 people during his span of service, being involved in some of the most dramatic rescues ever known. Happily, the tradition of selfless service is maintained. In 1970, another Cromer lifeboatman, Henry 'Shrimp' Davies, was also awarded the British Empire Medal.

PART THREE

USEFUL
INFORMATION

Transport

Rail
There are daily services from Norwich to Cromer and Sheringham. There is no station at Knettishall, but buses run from Bury St Edmunds station to Coney Weston. The Norwich–Ely line offers daily services to Thetford, while occasional trains stop at Brandon and Harling Road. From Brandon it is possible to walk the Harling Drove Road to join the Peddars Way at Bridgham Heath (9½ miles/15.3 km). Taxis are available from Thetford Station. National Rail Enquiries: 08457 484950.

Buses
Bus routes change frequently. Generally, the availability of bus routes is improving. Both Hunstanton and Cromer have National Express links. The Coast Path is served by the excellent Coast Hopper that runs throughout the year. The Peddars Way is rather more difficult at present. The best way to reach Knettishall is by bus from Bury St Edmunds. You will have to walk the 2 miles from Coney Weston to Knettishall. Details from Suffolk Bus Information: 08459 583358. For Norfolk services contact Norfolk Bus Information Centre: 08453 006116.

Car parking
A greater frequency of communities on the coast makes parking easier than on the Peddars Way, though some villages are a mile or two off the route. Many of the junctions created by country roads crossing the Peddars Way are not suitable, but occasional unmarked spaces can be found. Major parking areas along the trail are marked on the maps. At Knettishall there is a small parking area at the southern end of the route and another (locked at night) near the picnic area. Overnight parking is not recommended.

Accommodation

The bed and breakfast situation has improved in the last few years, but seasonal pressures, particularly near the coast, can create difficulties. The Way crosses a thinly populated landscape, while coastal communities tend to become crowded in summer. Book well in advance. Information can be obtained from TICs (see page 138). The Norfolk Ramblers' Association also produces an accommodation guide, which covers the complete route and includes current information on pubs, banks, shops and post offices. It can be purchased from some TICs or from the Association (see page 142).

Possible accommodation places include Thetford, Thompson, Little Cressingham, Watton, North Pickenham, Swaffham, Castle Acre, Great Massingham, Sedgeford, Hunstanton, Thornham, Brancaster, Overy Staithe, Wells, Stiffkey, Blakeney, Cley, Salthouse, Weybourne, Sheringham and Cromer.

There are YHA hostels at King's Lynn, some miles from the route, and at Hunstanton, Wells and Sheringham on the Trail. There is also a YHA hostel in Norwich. Information is available from the YHA. There is a Bunkhouse Barn at Courtyard Farm, Ringstead – grant-aided by the Countryside Commission and Norfolk County Council, it sleeps 12 and you will need a sleeping bag. For bookings contact: Courtyard Farm Bunkhouse Barn, Ringstead, Hunstanton, PE36 5IQ. A Bunkhouse Barn at Burnham Deepdale was opened in 1991. This is Deepdale Granary Bunkhouse Barn, which is a few yards south of the main coast road between Deepdale garage and the church. For bookings contact Deepdale Farm, Burnham Deepdale, King's Lynn, PE31 8DD. Tel. 01485 210256. Another hostel can be found at Castle Acre. This is the Old Red Lion, Bailey Street, Castle Acre, PE32 2AG. Tel. 01760 755557.

There are a few camping sites along the Peddars Way, and some farmers are willing to allow overnight camping on the basis of a personal enquiry. Camping is not permitted in Forestry Commission plantations. There is a short-stay backpackers' site at Knettishall (contact the warden). At the Forestry Commission's Thorpe Woodlands site a small area for backpackers is made available between April and late December (contact the warden). Sites are easier to find along the coast. General site information can be obtained from TICs or the Norfolk Ramblers' Association's accommodation guide.

Cromer's pier, with its theatre and lifeboat station, marks the end of the journey.

Tourist Information Centres

Tourist information centres (TICs) are useful for details of accommodation, transport and places to visit. There are four along the Trail – at Cromer, Hunstanton, Sheringham and Wells. Some have seasonal opening times.

Cromer TIC, Bus Station, Prince of Wales Road, Cromer, Norfolk, NR27 9HS. Tel. 01263 512497.

Hunstanton TIC, Town Hall, The Green, Hunstanton, Norfolk, PE36 6BQ. Tel. 01485 532610.

King's Lynn TIC, Custom House, Purfleet Quay, King's Lynn, Norfolk, PE30 1HP. Tel. 01553 763044.

Norwich TIC, The Forum, Millennium Plain, Norwich, Norfolk, NR2 1TF. Tel. 01603 727927.

Sheringham TIC, Station Approach, Sheringham, Norfolk, NR26 8RA. Tel. 01263 824329.

Swaffham TIC, Market Place, Swaffham, Norfolk, PE37 7AB. Tel. 01760 722255.

Wells-next-the-Sea TIC, Staithe Street, Wells-next-the-Sea, Norfolk, NR23 1AN. Tel. 01328 710885.

Local facilities

It is not practical to list local facilities, because rural communities are in a constant state of flux. In general, some villages along the Peddars Way have a shop, post office, pub or phone box, but not all. Along the coast most places have them. The larger places – Thetford, Watton, Swaffham, Hunstanton, Wells, Sheringham, Cromer – have most, if not all, facilities. One of the best markets is at Swaffham on Saturday morning.

	Early closing	Market day/s
Thetford	Weds	Tues, Sat
Watton	Thurs	Weds
Swaffham	Thurs	Sat
King's Lynn	Weds	Tues, Fri, Sat
Hunstanton	Thurs	Weds
Wells	Thurs	Weds
Sheringham	Weds	Sat
Cromer	Weds	Tues

Other walks

The 34-mile (54-km) Nar Valley Way links Gressenhall, near East Dereham, with King's Lynn, crossing the Peddars Way at Castle Acre. It joins the Wash Coast Path at Lynn.

The Weavers Way, from Cromer to Great Yarmouth, which passes through or by Felbrigg, Blickling, Aylsham, North Walsham, Halvergate Marsh and by Breydon Water, is a 57-mile (91-km) route on public footpaths, lengths of disused railway line and minor roads. Angles Way, the Broads to Brecks path, is a 77½-mile (125-km) route along the Waveney and Little Ouse valleys, linking Great Yarmouth with the Peddars Way at Knettishall.

The Weavers and Angles Way walks, with the Peddars Way and Coast Path, form an Around Norfolk Walk of about 220 miles (354 km).

Knettishall Country Park also links with the Icknield Way, which runs south through Royston and Luton to Ivinghoe Beacon, where the route also joins the Ridgeway National Trail (details from the Icknield Way Association). Thus it is possible to walk from Holme (Norfolk) to Avebury (Wiltshire), a distance of nearly 250 miles (400 km).

Details of all these walks and more are available from Norfolk County Council (see page 142).

Bridleways

Bridle paths along the Coast Path are short and fragmented and have not been included on our maps. The situation on the Peddars Way is better. Indeed, just about all of the Way north of Shepherd's Bush is bridleway. They are all waymarked with blue arrows.

One continuous route has been designed. It begins near the railway level crossing at Bridgham Heath and follows sections of the Peddars Way to Holme, taking in Cockley Cley, the Fincham Drove Road and West Acre. A leaflet, *Peddars Way: a route for horseriders*, is obtainable from the National Trail Office.

Cycling

Cycling must be restricted to bridleway (waymarked with blue arrows) and road sections. The coastal section is 'out of bounds', but there is a Norfolk Coast Cycleway leaflet available from Tourist Information Centres. Much of the Peddars Way can be cycled although there are three sections where bicycles are not allowed because of the footpath status. Contact the National Trail Office for more details.

Equal access

Equal access is something that the managing authorities take seriously. There is a continuous programme of improvements, both to the physical route and in the information supplied. The long-term aim is to produce both printed and web-based information that will enable those with special needs to find out what the barriers are before visiting the Trail. To speak to someone who knows the physical route, contact the National Trails Manager.

Trail management

The Trail is managed by a partnership of local authorities and the Countryside Agency. Day-to-day management is discharged through the National Trail Manager.

Useful addresses

Breckland Council, The Guildhall, St Withburga Lane, East Dereham, Norfolk, NR19 1EE. Tel. 01363 695333.

Coastguard Maritime Rescue Co-ordination Centre, 4th Floor, Haven Bridge House, Great Yarmouth, Norfolk, NR30 1HZ. Tel. weather and tides information 01493 851338. (In an emergency, dial 999 and ask for the Coastguard.)

Countryside Agency, Eastern Regional Office, Ortona House, 110 Hills Road, Cambridge, CB2 1LQ. Tel. 01223 354462. Website: www.countryside.gov.uk

East of England Tourist Board, Toppesfield Hall, Hadleigh, Suffolk, IP7 5DN. Tel. 01473 822922.

English Nature, Regional Office, 60 Bracondale, Norwich, NR1 2BE. Tel. 01603 620558.

Enthusiasts of steam can wallow in nostalgia at Sheringham's North Norfolk Railway.

First Eastern Counties Omnibus Co. Ltd, Bus Enquiries, Bus Station, Surrey Street, Norwich, NR1 3NX. Tel. 08456 020121.

Forest Enterprise, District Office, Santon Downham, Brandon, IP27 0TJ. Tel. 01842 810271.

Icknield Way Association, 19 Boundary Road, Bishops Stortford, Herts. CM23 5LE.

King's Lynn and West Norfolk Borough Council, King's Court, Queen Street, King's Lynn, PE30 1EX. Tel. 01553 692722.

Knettishall Heath Country Park Warden. Tel. 01953 688265.

National Trail Office, 6 Station Road, Wells, Norfolk, NR23 1AE. Tel. 01328 711533. Email: peddars.way@dial.pipex.com

National Trust, East Anglia Regional Office, Blickling, Norwich, NR11 6NF. Tel. 01263 733471.

Norfolk Bus Information Centre: Local call 08453 006116.

Norfolk Coast AONB Partnership, 6 Station Road, Wells, Norfolk, NR23 1AE. Website: www.norfolkcoastaonb.org.uk

Norfolk County Council, County Hall, Martineau Lane, Norwich, NR1 2SG. Tel. 01603 222222. Public Rights of Way enquiries tel. 01603 223284. Website: www.norfolk.gov.uk

Norfolk Wildlife Trust, 72 Cathedral Close, Norwich, NR1 4DF. Tel. 01603 625540.

North Norfolk District Council, Holt Road, Cromer, NR27 9DZ. Tel. 01263 513811.

Ordnance Survey, Romsey Road, Maybush, Southampton, SO16 4GU. Tel. 08456 050505. Website: www.ordsvy.gov.uk

Ramblers' Association, Norfolk Area, 111 Belvoir Street, Norwich, NR2 3AZ. Tel. 01603 663029.

Royal Society for the Protection of Birds, East Anglian Office, Stalham House, 65 Thorpe Road, Norwich, NR1 1UD. Tel. 01603 661662.

Thorpe Woodlands Camp Site Warden. Tel. 01842 751042.

Youth Hostels Association, South England Region, 116 York Road, Salisbury, Wilts, SP2 7AP. Tel. 01722 337494.

Bibliography

General

Bridgwater, Elizabeth, *Bridgwater's Norfolk*. (Encompass Press, 1995).

Clarke, R. Rainbird, *In Breckland Wilds* (EP Publishing Ltd, republished 1974).

East Anglia Guide (East Anglia Tourist Board, annually).

Mason, H. J. and McClelland, A., *Background to Breckland*, (Providence Press, 1994).

Pocock, Tom, *Norfolk* (Pimlico, 1995).

Scott, Clement, *Poppyland* (reprinted, Christine Stockwell, 1992).

Natural history

Clarke, Peter and Helen, *Where to Watch Birds in East Anglia* (Christopher Helm, 1988).

Norfolk Wildlife Trust, *The Reserves Handbook* (Norfolk Wildlife Trust, 1995).

Wilson, Ron, *Norfolk in The Four Seasons* (The Lark's Press, 1995).

Churches

Mortlock, D. P. and Roberts, C. V., *The Popular Guide to Norfolk Churches*, Nos 1 (North-East Norfolk) and 3 (West and South-West Norfolk) (Acorn Editions, 1981 and 1985).

Lifeboats

Poppyland Publishing has produced a series of booklets on Norfolk's lifeboats including: *Hunstanton* (by Stibbons, T., 1984), *Sheringham* (Malster, R. W., 1981) and *Cromer* (Malster, R. W. and Stibbons, P., 1986).

History

Dymond, David, *The Norfolk Landscape* (Hodder & Stoughton, 1985).

Hibbert, Christopher, *Nelson* (Viking, 1994).

Museums Service, Norfolk, *Norfolk From the Air* (Norfolk Museums Service, 1987).

Robinson, Bruce and Rose, Edwin J., *Norfolk Origins 2: Roads and Tracks* (Poppyland Publishing, 1982).

— and Gregory, Tony, *Norfolk Origins 3: Celtic Fire and Roman Rule* (Poppyland Publishing, 1987).

Skipper, Kate and Williamson, Tom, *The Angles Way* (Centre of East Anglian Studies, 1993).

Wade Martins, Peter, *An Historical Atlas of Norfolk* (Norfolk Museums Service, 1993).

Wade Martins, Susanna, *A History of Norfolk* (Phillimore, 1984).

Williamson, Tom, *The Origins of Norfolk* (Manchester University Press, 1993).

Ordnance Survey Maps covering the Peddars Way and Norfolk Coast Path

Landranger Maps (scale: 1:50 000): 132, 133, 144

Pathfinder Maps (scale: 1:25 000): 818 (TF64/74), 819 (TF84/91), 820 (TG04/14), 839 (TF63/73), 842 (TG23/33), 859 (TF62/72), 880 (TF61/71), 881 (TF81/91), 901 (TF80/90), 922 (TL89/99), 943 (TL88/98)

Explorer Maps (scale 1:25 000): 23, 24, 25, 229, 230 and 236.

Motoring Maps: Reach the Peddars Way and Norfolk Coast Path using Travelmaster Maps (scale: 1:250 000) 6, 'East Midlands and East Anglia', and 9, 'South East England'.

The Coastal Code

- Look out for signs and leaflets showing how to prevent damage to sensitive coastal wildlife
- Reduce erosion of fragile habitats by keeping to paths and established routes
- Avoid disturbance of birds and other animals; seals and shorebirds are particularly vulnerable
- Keep dogs under close control or on a lead
- Leave wild flowers for others to enjoy
- Play and sit on the beach not the dunes
- Reduce the risk of fire by not lighting fires, stoves or barbecues
- Take your litter home
- Use your bicycle but stick to authorised routes
- Shop locally